1999 ED

201 *Easy* Ways

TO

REDUCE
YOUR
TAXES

EVELYN JACKS

McGraw-Hill
Ryerson

Toronto   Montreal   New York   Burr Ridge   Bangkok   Bogotá
Caracas   Lisbon   London   Madrid   Mexico City   Milan   New Delhi
Seoul   Singapore   Sydney   Taipei

McGraw-Hill
Ryerson Limited

A Subsidiary of The McGraw·Hill Companies

300 Water Street, Whitby, Ontario, L1N 9B6
http://www.mcgrawhill.ca

201 Easy Ways to Reduce Your Taxes
Copyright © 1999 by The Jacks Institute
Previous editions published as 201 Ways to Reduce Your Taxes © 1997, 1996 by Evelyn Jacks
Jacks' Tax Tips © 1995, 1994 by Evelyn Jacks

ISBN: 0-07-560541-4

1 2 3 4 5 6 7 8 9 10   W   7 6 5 4 3 2 1 0 9 8
Printed and bound in Canada

This book has been meticulously researched and compiled using the latest information available from Revenue Canada and the Department of Finance at the time of writing. Because tax and filing procedures are continually changing the author and publisher cannot be responsible for errors or omissions. We welcome any information that enables us to clarify or expand on issues of interest to our readers.

This book is sold with the understanding that neither the author nor the publisher is hereby rendering legal, accounting, or other professional advice. If such advice or other assistance is required, the personal services of a competent professional should be sought.

Canadian Cataloguing in Publication Data
Jacks, Evelyn, 1955-
    201 ways to reduce your taxes

Annual
1996 ed.-
Continues: Jacks, Evelyn, 1955-   . Jacks' tax tips, ISSN 1200-3832.
ISBN 0-07-560541-4 (1999)
ISBN 1204-556X

1. Income tax – Law and legislation – Canada – Popular works. 2. Tax planning – Canada – Popular works. I. Title. II. Title: Reduce your taxes.

HJ4661.A2J33   343.7105'2'05   C96-300293-7

Publisher: Joan Homewood
Coordinating Editor: Catherine Leek
Production Coordinator: Susanne Penny
Cover design: Jack Steiner
Editorial services: Rachel Mansfield
Page design/composition: Lynda Powell

For Peter and Gabrielle
A special thought
for two special people

"The triumph of life is
expressed by creation"
Henri Bergson

ABOUT EVELYN JACKS

Evelyn Jacks is Founder and President of **The Jacks Institute**, a national private career college specializing in tax and business-related courses for individuals and tax industry professionals. She is the author of over 20 best-selling books on personal income tax preparation, and over 70 industry-related training courses. Evelyn is a frequent national commentator on federal and provincial budgets and has criss-crossed Canada for over a dozen years to answer your tax questions on local and national TV and radio programs.

Other books by Evelyn Jacks:

Jacks on Tax Savings: Everyone's Favourite Canadian Tax Guide to Preparing Income Tax Returns. 15th Anniversary Edition.

The Complete Canadian Home Business Guide to Taxes. 3rd edition.

Jacks on Personal Finance: Modern Money Management for Utterly Confused Canadians. 1st edition.

Jacks on GST: The Authoritative Guide for Business and Consumers.

Certificate Courses from The Jacks Institute: These home study courses feature software by CANTAX, Hometax, *L'Impôt Personnel*; while book-keeping/payroll courses feature software by *Simply Accounting*.

The Career Builder programs include:

The Quick and Easy Tax Course for Beginners: a simple income tax preparation course for beginners designed to train students to prepare their own income tax returns by computer, or those of friends and family.

The Intermediate Personal Income Tax Preparation Course: a professional entry level course designed to train the student to prepare professional computerized tax returns for others, out of home or office, or gain employment within the financial services industry.

The Computerized Advanced Income Tax Preparation Course: an advanced course for experienced professionals who wish to enhance tax preparation techniques and do tax planning scenarios by computer.

The Small Business Tax Course: for unincorporated business ventures, a detailed course on tax filing provisions including statement preparation, capital acquisitions and dispositions, income and operational deductions.

The Computerized Payroll Clerk Course: a skill-oriented course that teaches payroll cheque distribution, T4 Slip preparation, and month end reporting with an emphasis on tax obligations of the employer and employee.

The Computerized Bookkeeping Course for Small Business: learn how to prepare books by computer for small business enterprises.

The Jacks on Tax Update Newsletter Service: quarterly reports on significant personal tax changes throughout the year.

CONTENTS

INTRODUCTION

Tax Season 1999: the last one before the turn of the century. What will the 21st century bring to Canadian taxpayers? Continued change is a safe bet, and, according to recent fiscal trends, some good news too.

Deficit spending, it appears, has been conquered in Canada. The February 24, 1998, federal budget has brought us joyful news: for the years 1997 to 2000 the federal government will stop adding to our 583 billion dollar debt, and produce a financial surplus. This has only been achieved a handful of times since 1926. The combination of balanced budgeting and debt reduction could spell tax relief. For some low- and middle-income earners, this will come to pass on the 1998 tax return. Yet, in 1999-2000 the federal government will still collect more taxes: a 3.8% increase over the prior year. One reason for the increase is "bracket creep," the fact that tax rates are not fully indexed to inflation. The Canadian tax system is successfully progressive; which means, the more money you make, the more you'll pay.

In fact, the top 30% of Canadian income earners pay 63.9% of all taxes, while the bottom 30%, pay only 5.2% of all taxes. That leaves the 40% in the middle, who earn about 34% of all income, to pay about 31% of all taxes. (*The Fraser Forum, July 1998*)

Therefore, people at different income levels have different tax-filing — and tax-planning — objectives. Those at the lower-income levels will want to file a return to reap rewards from income re-distribution: the refundable tax credits and non-refundable tax benefits put in place especially for them.

The highest-income earners will want to plan to defer taxation into the future, when savings must be tapped to finance old age, hopefully at lower marginal tax rates.

And the middle class will find that they have the most to lose from poor tax preparation and tax planning. Over-reporting income or understating deductions could result in the clawback or elimination of social benefits such as the GST Credit, the Child Tax Benefits, Employment Insurance or OAS. These clawbacks result in marginally higher tax rates for some middle-income earners compared to top-income earners.

Therefore, when it comes to your taxes, a little extra knowledge can be a valuable commodity. Even if you choose never to file your own tax return, knowing more about your tax-filing rights will help you ask the right questions of your professional advisors, and hopefully reap more of the new "fiscal dividend" the government has produced — and promised.

That is the purpose of this little book: to share a little knowledge, in an easy-to-read style, which hopefully will help you achieve the peace of mind that comes with knowing that you have paid only the correct amount of tax, now and over your lifetime...and not one cent more!

Evelyn Jacks

TOP 20 TAX CHANGES

There are numerous changes to the 1998 tax return. Here are the top 20:

1. **Individual Surtax Reductions:** The 3% individual surtax will be reduced by up to $125 in 1998 and $250 in 1999. Income levels and non-refundable credits will determine the reduction amount.

2. **New Personal Amount Supplement:** The Tax-Free Zone increases for low-income earners by up to $250 more in 1998 and $500 in 1999. This will depend on net income levels and affect numerous calculations, including the claim for tuition and education credits, and the Spousal Transfers.

3. **Provincial Tax Rates Drop:** Tax relief abounds for residents of B.C., Alberta, Saskatchewan, Manitoba, Ontario, New Brunswick and Nova Scotia.

4. **Canada Child Tax Benefits:** As a result of a new federal-provincial initiative additional Child Tax Benefits, administered by Revenue Canada, are now also available in the following provinces: B.C., Alberta, Saskatchewan, New Brunswick, Nova Scotia and the Northwest Territories. Filing a return for families is a must!

5. **Severance Packages:** Those who receive severance packages will no longer be subject to minimum tax if these funds are transferred to an RRSP (retroactive to settlements received after 1993).

6. **Good News for Students:** Education Tax Credits have increased for full-time students to $200 a month; a new $60 a month education tax credit is also available for some part-time students. (One or the other may be claimed in a given month.) Note that the part-time credit may affect the claim for child care expenses on Line 214. The Student Loan Interest Credit also gives tax relief to those with student loans.

7. **RESP Withdrawals:** A contributor may now make an RESP income withdrawal in certain cases, which must be included in income, subject to a special tax of 20% over and above that individual's normal marginal tax rate, unless the amounts are rolled into an RRSP. Sufficient RRSP Room must be available.

8. **RESP Contributions:** The federal government will provide a Canada Education Savings Grant of 20% of the first $2,000 deposited to an RESP for qualifying beneficiaries, starting in 1998.

9. **Auto Write-Offs Increase:** Employees or the self-employed who use their cars in their work will be pleased to know of the increase in deductions for leasing or capital cost allowances in 1998.

10. **Child Care Expenses:** Maximum child care deduction ceilings have been increased to $7,000 for each child under 7 or severely disabled, and $4,000 for children age 7-16, while weekly amounts generally claimed by higher-income earners have increased too. Special claims can also be made in cases where parents go to school either full-time or part-time.

11. **Moving Expenses:** Deductible expenses now include certain costs of carrying an unsold residence.

12. **Employment Benefits:** Employer-funded training is now tax-free, unless payment is provided for courses taken for self-interest, unrelated to the employer's business. But employees who receive other benefits from their employers, such as help with the financing of a new residence or losses on the sale of an old residence, must include those benefits in taxable income.

13. **New Caregivers' Tax Credit:** Available to those who take care of a parent or grandparent aged 65 years or older, or an adult relative who is dependent due to mental or physical infirmity, if the dependant's income is below $13,853.

14. **Disability Amount:** This lucrative credit is now claimable based on the verification of disability by licensed medical practitioners, now including occupational therapists and psychologists.

15. **Medical Expenses:** Costs of training courses taken to better care for an infirm dependant are now allowed.

16. **CSB News:** In 1998 Series 43 matured and must be reported for the final time. Report Series 44 on the triennial method.

17. **Emergency Services:** Tax savings increase for volunteer emergency services personnel, who now qualify for a deduction of up to $1,000 against income received, providing a prescribed form is filed.

18. **Small Business News**: There is a new tax deduction for group health premiums, if they meet certain income and staffing requirements. There are also some restrictions in claiming meals and entertainment for staff, and a new accelerated tax deduction for small businesses investing to upgrade computer systems for Year 2000 compliance. A fourth-year reserve calculation applies to those who changed their income reporting methods to a calendar year end in 1995.

19. **U.S. Social Security Benefits:** New reporting rules require reporting of all retirement benefits received, in Canadian funds, with an offsetting tax deduction of 15% on Line 256 of the Canadian return.

20. **Labour-Sponsored Funds Tax Credit:** The maximum annual federal credit has increased to 15% of a maximum investment of $5,000, for a maximum federal credit of $750 in 1998.

WHY TAX PLANNING REALLY PAYS OFF

Do you know...

* *You can significantly increase monthly family income simply by filing a tax return...*
* *You should prepare family tax returns starting with the lowest-income earner...*
* *There are legal ways to reduce tax by transferring income from higher earner to lower earner...*
* *Every family member should file a return every year...*

The objective of tax planning is to legally minimize the amount of tax you pay by arranging your affairs within the framework of the law so that you'll pay the least amount possible. This is your right and duty as a Canadian taxpayer.

When it comes to income taxes though, many squander this right, citing the fact that their eyes glaze over at the mere mention of the word "tax."

This has always puzzled me, as most people do understand that tax savings and real money are one and the same.

It often helps to see "the Big Picture." Think about it: how much tax do you pay each year? Now, project this number forward to arrive at your "lifetime tax obligation." You probably got a very big number, right?

Did you know that the average family of four pays taxes of over $33,000 every year, at a tax rate of 48.2%?* Over a productive lifetime of 40 years, this family is paying $1,320,000 in taxes to governments of Canada. Quite an eye-opener, isn't it?

Let's take this fact a step further. Are you sure that you and your family are taking advantage of each and every tax deduction and tax credit you are entitled to? Just think, by ensuring that all tax provisions available to you are used every year, and by planning to reduce your tax burden, you could shave perhaps 10%, 15% or more off your annual tax burden. In the case of the average family listed above, this could reap $132,000 to $198,000 or more in real tax dollar savings over the 40-year period.

Most taxpayers' interests are aroused when they anticipate six-figure tax savings over their lifetimes. They dream about an easier life in the cottage of their dreams, paying off their mortgages sooner, or taking those winter vacations many Canadians strive for.

Turning dreams into reality can be as simple as taking control of your lifetime income tax bill. And it's easier than you might think. Like any new subject area, though, you'll need to become familiar with a couple of key concepts.

For example, you'll need to take the time to understand the basic elements of a tax return. Yes, that means you'll actually have to take a look at the darn thing, and at least know where to find the lines that tell you these things:

- your total income
- your net income
- your taxable income
- your taxes payable
- the amount of tax you have already paid through source deductions or instalment.

Remember that for some Canadians, filing a tax return is also an application for new monthly income. Our tax system does more than just collect taxes; it also redistributes income to the poor and working poor. Even if you or an adult family member have little or no income, a tax return should be filed to take advantage of various refundable federal and provincial tax credits.

Next you'll need to clue in to asking certain tax questions before you make financial decisions. For example, you'll want to find out how the new child support payment guidelines impact your children's standard of living, or how the equity holdings within your non-registered mutual fund account compare to your Canada Savings Bonds—

---

* The Fraser Institute, 1998.

after tax. To do these things, you'll need to keep up to date on personal tax changes from year to year.

Finally, you'll need to take a long-term tax view. If you can plan your future income and capital accumulations with an eye to tax efficiency, you'll accumulate more wealth. Tax planning, then, is an integral part of ensuring that you pay the least under our tax system and reap the most from your personal productivity.

Almost every Canadian can benefit from a little tax knowledge. That's why we suggest that you...

 1 BEGIN YOUR TAX PLANNING ACTIVITIES TODAY

Tax planning involves a multi-year approach to your tax-filing routine. To make a commitment to reducing your tax bill, follow these eight Key Tax Planning Steps:

- Know the effective or actual rate of taxes you are paying on your total income this year.
- Know the tax rate on the next dollar you will earn.
- Know how different income sources are taxed.
- Know the *new* "Tax-Free Income Zone" for each family member.
- Know how to transfer income to spouse and children.
- Know how to defer income and taxes into the future.
- Know how to maximize each tax provision that could apply to your family.
- Know how to recover overpaid taxes of prior years.

 2 COMPUTE YOUR EFFECTIVE TAX RATE

In Canada today we have three federal tax rates, and a "Tax-Free Zone." The tax-free zone is the amount of money you can make before paying any taxes at all. For most people this is a combination of their tax deductions and non-refundable tax credits. However, for all taxpayers, the tax-free zone amounts to the Basic Personal Amount of $6,456 plus, starting in 1998, a supplement to this amount of up to $250 more.* For most low-income earners, then, The Tax-Free Zone will be $6,706 in 1998.

In every province but Quebec, the federal government also collects taxes on behalf of the provinces. The following chart shows how federal taxes are collected on taxable income:

---

* This was increased to $500 for 1998.

Taxable Income	Federal Tax Rate
Less than $6,707	nil
Up to $29,590	17%
$29,591 to $59,180	26%
Over $59,180	29%

To compute your actual tax rate on current income, dig out your most current tax return and find Line 435 on your tax return. This is total federal and provincial taxes payable for the year. Divide this number by your total income on Line 150. The result is your effective tax rate on total income sources. That's where you stand today.

Example: Line 435 is $10,000 and Line 150 is $42,000. Your effective tax rate on total income is 23.8%

 3   KNOW HOW TO COMPUTE YOUR MARGINAL TAX RATE

How much tax will you pay on the next dollar you earn? In our example above, for a single taxpayer working as an employee in Ontario, a salary increase will be taxed at a marginal rate of about 37%. That's a far cry from the effective or actual tax rate. Why?

Because our tax system is progressive, the more income a taxpayer makes, the more s/he pays. The effective tax rate previously calculated takes into account the "Tax-Free Zone" allowed to each taxpayer, which includes the Basic Personal Amounts and the new Personal Amount Supplement. It takes into account the lower taxes applied to incomes at the lower brackets.

As your income increases, the tax you pay on the next dollar is proportionately greater, and the benefit of tax credits can be eroded, clawed back or eliminated entirely. That is why it's important to know your current marginal tax rate, and how you might be able to reduce it.

Example: Mary, a single resident of Ontario aged 66, earns $4,900 from her Old Age Security, $7,500 from Canada Pension Plan and $15,000 from her company pension. She has accumulated $100,000 in an RRSP and wants to start taking a periodic pension from this. Mary's current marginal tax rate is about 27.5%, as she is still in the lower tax bracket. The chart below shows how the marginal tax rates increase at different income levels. This will help Mary plan her RRIF pension level:

Marginal Tax Rate (1998) for Mary

Taxable Income:	$27,400	$37,400	$67,400
Tax Rate:	27.5%	40%	50%

4 KNOW HOW DIFFERENT INCOME SOURCES ARE TAXED

Most Canadians are unaware that different income sources are taxed at different tax rates. For example, you will pay tax at the highest marginal rates on the following income sources:

- salary, bonus, vacation pay and taxable benefits
- pensions from private or public sources
- Employment Insurance benefits
- interest income.

However certain income sources qualify for "tax preferences" under the Income Tax Act:

- dividends from Canadian companies
- capital gains
- rental income (only net income after deductions is taxed)
- business income (only net income after deductions is taxed)
- scholarships, fellowships and bursaries (the first $500 is tax exempt)
- social benefits like Workers' Compensation, Social Assistance Payments and Federal Supplements
- retiring allowances rolled over into RRSPs.

Other income sources are not subject to tax and need not be reported at all. These include:

- profits from the sale of your principal residence
- life insurance policy proceeds
- inheritances received
- certain benefits of employment, like membership to an athletic club, or discounts on merchandise.

Income diversification, then, is a key to minimization of tax.

 # 5 KNOW THE TAX-FREE ZONE FOR EACH FAMILY MEMBER

As mentioned, the Canadian tax system allows each family member to earn a certain amount of money before tax rates apply. For the past several years, the basic tax-free zone has been marked by the Basic Personal Amount: $6456 for the year or $538 per month.

For 1998, the February 24, 1998 federal budget announced a Personal Amount Supplement of $250; in 1999 this will go up to $500. This means that in 1999 and future years, the lowest-income earners in the country can make just under $580 a month before any taxes are payable.

It is important to know this, as you can then plan to split income with family members, or devise RRSP contribution plans for each part-time worker, to ensure that the Tax-Free Zone is maximized each year, if possible.

6 KNOW HOW TO TRANSFER INCOME TO SPOUSE AND KIDS

One of the best ways to minimize the tax you pay is to try to transfer income from the higher-income earner to the lower earners in the family. This is called "income splitting." However, one must be very careful not to invoke the "Attribution Rules."

The Attribution Rules ensure that when certain assets are transferred from a high-earning spouse to the lower-earning spouse or child, resulting income is taxed back to the high-income earner. If, for example, you transfer interest-bearing investments, such as a Canada Savings Bond, to your spouse, or a child who is under 18 years of age, the resulting earnings will be taxed back to you. But there are ways to legally circumvent these Attribution Rules. These are discussed at length in Chapter 3.

7 KNOW HOW TO DEFER INCOME AND TAXES INTO THE FUTURE

The more your income grows, the higher your rate of tax. This is a simple tax concept. In addition, the more money you have, the greater the chances are that you will have some disposable dollars; that is, money left over after all necessities of life are covered.

When you have disposable income, the key is to defer taxation into the future, when you'll need to tap those dollars for living expenses. One way to do this is to diversify your investments.

Generally you will try to invest disposable income in an RRSP first, as such investments give you two financial rewards. The first is a tax deduction in the amount of the principal invested, provided you have followed the "RRSP Room" guidelines. That is, you can only invest a certain percentage of income earned, and these earning must be adjusted for any contributions you make to a company pension plan. Check your Notice of Assessment from Revenue Canada to determine RRSP Room. (Note RC's figure will be inaccurate if you haven't filed a return to report actively earned income sources in the period 1990 to 1997.)

If you have enough money then also to invest outside an RRSP, you should know that dividends earned will be taxed at a preferred rate, and that capital gains are never taxed until disposition. From a tax viewpoint, investing in capital assets will help you accumulate wealth — without taxation — until you tap the source. This can give you some control over the timing of your tax burden.

8 CHOOSE INCOME REPORTING DATES WISELY

Individual taxpayers must report most income on a cash basis; that is, when received in the calendar year, January to December. Generally, when you transfer income from a year of high earnings to a year of lower earnings you will reap tax rewards.

Mike and Maureen, for example, own a duplex that they use as a rental property. In order to meet their financial commitments, they are considering selling it. They know that 75% of their expected profit of $35,000 each will be added to their income in the year of sale. With proper planning, timing, and the presence of a willing purchaser, this couple may be able to cut down their tax liability by selling one half of the duplex late this year and the other half early next year.

In another example, Meg and Matthew are expecting their first child in the spring. Meg will be staying home from work until the end of that tax year, after the baby is born. This might be a good tax year in which to realize capital gains income from the sale of an asset, or to make an RRSP withdrawal, as the income would be taxed at Meg's lower marginal rate.

The idea is to keep as much of the income as possible in the lowest tax bracket. This can be accomplished in some cases by reporting the income over two tax years, or by deferring the reporting of other income to a year of lower earnings.

9 CREATE RRSP ROOM

Earnings from employment or self-employment, net rental income, and even certain maintenance or alimony payments made under agreements in place before May 1, 1997, will qualify as "earned income" for RRSP purposes.

Contributing to the RRSP may have little benefit this year if you are not taxable. However, you may carry forward any undeducted contributions for use in the future. As well, RRSP contribution "room" can be carried forward *on an indefinite basis* to future tax years when income may be higher. Therefore, filing a tax return — even when you have a small income — may create a "future tax deduction" to offset income at that time. That can save you big dollars!

10 KNOW HOW TO MAXIMIZE EACH TAX PROVISION THAT COULD APPLY TO YOU

It is important to start keeping track of the tax changes that apply to you and your family. There is a bit of a learning curve, but it's not a treacherous mountain of unintelligible legalese.

Start by reading the Top 20 Tax Changes for of 1998 at the start of this book. Do any of them apply to you? If so, find out more. Ask your tax professional, call Revenue Canada, or consult our detailed line-by-line tax-filing guide, *Jacks on Tax Savings*. In this way, you won't miss out on the tax provisions that apply to you today.

Next, find the tax provisions that apply to you on the income tax return itself. (We'll help you identify these areas in the next section of this book.)

Then make a point of keeping up with personal tax changes that peak your interest. . .chances are they may affect a decision you are contemplating.

And remember *The Evelyn Jacks Rule of Thumb* when you're confused about whether a tax provision applies to you: There's no such thing as a stupid tax question! It's your money, you earned it. Make sure you know how to keep as much as you can in your own pocket.

11 REVIEW PRIOR-FILED TAX RETURNS

Always have a copy of tax returns for the immediate prior tax year on hand. This will allow you to preview any changes in your "taxpayer profile" by making a list of personal or financial circumstances that have occurred during the most recent tax year. You will also be prompted to send for the auxiliary tax forms from Revenue Canada, or to move from a "short form" such as the T1 Special to the T1 General Return should you have a more complicated tax situation this year.

You will also be alerted to any missed tax provisions. These can be recovered in most circumstances for each tax year as far back as 1985, simply by requesting an adjustment to your prior-filed returns. Revenue Canada provides a special form for this purpose, called a T1ADJ.

12 RECAPTURE PREVIOUSLY OVERPAID TAXES

You now know that taxpayers can request an adjustment to a prior-filed tax return, or recover tax refunds for missed returns of prior years, all the way back to 1985. This is a great way to recover new disposable income, when you're in a cash flow pinch.

For example, if you forgot to claim your annual safety deposit box fee of $65 a year, over a ten-year period, you will have missed $650 worth of legitimate tax deductions. This translates into $273 in overpaid taxes at a 42% marginal tax rate, or $27.30 each year. All it takes is a letter to the tax department to recoup your losses. Others may have forgotten to claim the old Federal Sales Tax Credit (see below).

If you didn't file a return in the past and you suspect you may have money coming back from refundable tax credits or overpaid source deductions, file the tax return(s) in question now. Revenue Canada won't send a refund to you unless you ask for it.

13 RECOVER THE OLD FEDERAL SALES TAX CREDIT

In 1991, the Federal Sales Tax Credit was discontinued. However, it is important to note that taxpayers may file to recover missed credits. At risk of missing out were those who turned 19 in the year or low-income seniors. A summary of refundable credits and income thresholds follows:

Federal Sales Tax Credit	1986	1987	1988	1989	1990
Per Adult	$50	$50	$70	$100	$140
Per Child	$25	$25	$35	$50	$70
Net Income Threshold	$15,000	$15,000	$16,000	$16,000	$18,000

If this happened to you write a letter to Revenue Canada requesting the Federal Sales Tax Credit to be sent to you for each year in which you were eligible.

14 FORCE YOURSELF TO INVEST YOUR TAX SAVINGS

For many taxpayers, the income tax refund is one of the largest capital receipts of the year.

Through electronic filing capabilities, you can have the money deposited directly into your bank account, under the general principle that "What can't be seen can't be spent!" Then, invest your tax refund wisely. A portion of the new funds could also be used to pay down your mortgage, credit card balances or other debts whose interest charges are non-deductible. The rest of the funds could be used to create new money; that is, by topping up your RRSP first, if you qualify to make contributions, and then other "non-registered" investments.

It's possible Grandma really had something in that saying, "A penny saved is a penny earned."

15 RETHINK YOUR SPENDING DECISIONS

One of the main reasons that taxpayers miss claiming tax deductions or credits is a lack of appreciation of the benefits a tax viewpoint can have on decision making. The wise tax planner won't make any personal or financial decision without considering all tax-planning alternatives first.

Sam, a young lawyer, is in the market for a new car. He wants a Mercedes. He can afford a moped.

With his dream in the background, he contemplates an important decision: Do I buy a new or used car? First, he considers the tax implications of leasing or buying the vehicle. (See Chapter 5 for more details.) Then, he steps outside this mindset to assess carefully the alternative uses for his money.

After much deliberation, Sam buys a used North American car.

He then takes the difference in savings between the new and used car costs and splits them in two ways: one-third of the money is salted away in an investment fund for safekeeping to be used for future repairs, as the used car has no warranty. The earnings on this investment also finance the annual licence and insurance fees.

Two-thirds of the savings are invested in Sam's RRSP. At his current marginal tax rate, this reaps a tax saving of 48% of his principal investment, which he receives in just three weeks after electronically filing his tax return. These savings are invested in another fund that Sam nicknames "The Mercedes Fund." Every year his tax savings from the RRSP investment add to the fund, which can be used to finance a downpayment for the car.

Sam soon finds the need to reassess his options in light of the rapidly accumulating Mercedes Fund. Does he really want the luxury car, or is there a better investment-oriented decision he can make?

Funny thing about money — it's always either in your pocket, or someone else's. Used as a tool to create wealth, Sam will get better mileage from his after-tax dollar.

16 SPREAD THE WEALTH WITHIN THE FAMILY

In most families, the higher-income earner typically invests money, and the lower earner spends part-time earnings or social benefit payments, such as tax refunds or the Goods and Services Tax Credit, on consumer goods.

Consider, for a moment, the benefit of the opposite strategy: if the lower-income earner invested social benefit payments or other income sources received, the investment earnings on those principal amounts would be included in that person's income.

The result: more of the investment income would stay in the family because it would be taxed at a lower tax rate, if at all.

It makes sense to use a tax focus when making decisions about your money. For example, use the monies earned by the higher earner to maximize an RRSP investment, as this will reap progressively higher tax benefits the higher your tax bracket.

RRSP deposit decisions can also lead to tax-wise income-splitting. By making the RRSP contribution in the name of the lower-earning spouse, subsequent withdrawals in retirement will be taxed at the lower earner's tax rate, provided certain holding requirements are met.

Lower earners who are taxable should also consider making an RRSP contribution, if they have RRSP "room." The resulting lower net income might create higher Child Tax Benefit or GST Credit returns, a higher new Refundable Medical Expense Supplement, or additional deductions or credits for the higher-income earner.

Wealth creation and wealth preservation can be multiplied if you involve every family member.

CHAPTER 2

KEY TAX PREPARATION TIPS

Do you know...

* *Filing an accurate tax return is the first step in reaping tax savings...*
* *Most taxpayers don't know the lucrative tax deductions they are entitled to...*
* *Deductions missed in previous years can be easily recovered...*
* *Planning a move to another province can bring you a tax refund windfall...*
* *Medical expenses are often missed...*

Someone once said that nothing is too difficult if you break it down into parts. That principle certainly holds true when it comes to income tax preparation. Most people know and understand that they must file a tax return every year, or face financial consequences. In fact, the tax-filing deadline is usually the prime motivating factor most people have in facing this subject at all! Truth is, tax-filing time is no time to plan to reduce the level of your tax bill. . . when you file this year's return, you're basically recording history. To minimize your lifetime tax bill, it is the planning you do throughout the year that will reap for you the kind of tax savings you might think your neighbours are getting. What do they know that you don't?

There are a few basic parameters that every taxpayer should know about filing their tax return. We'll let you in on a few of these "secrets."

17 USE THE T1 GENERAL TAX FORM

Despite Revenue Canada's attempts to simplify the tax return, Canadians who really want to be sure they are claiming every tax deduction and credit they are entitled to should use the T1 General Tax Form. This is the only tax form that makes reference to all the tax deductions, tax credits and tax calculations to which you are entitled. Knowledge about this form also makes the transition to computer tax software use easier.

18 KNOW WHO MUST FILE

You are required to file a tax return if you owe the government money for the tax year; or if you disposed of a capital property, such as a cottage or mutual fund. You must file if you are wishing to receive Old Age Security pension in the future or if Canada Pension Plan contributions are required on your self-employment profits. Revenue Canada may send you a formal request to file, in which case you must file a tax return.

You will want to file to claim refunds owed to you or to file for refundable tax credits, such as the Goods and Services Tax Credit, or certain carry-over provisions. Filing on time can also create handsome monthly "returns" for your family. For example, both spouses must file a tax return in order to receive the monthly Child Tax Benefit for children under the age of 19.

19 KNOW HOW TO DO IT YOURSELF IN SIX EASY STEPS

There are several key figures on the tax return that will affect the amount of tax you pay and whether you qualify for a refundable tax credit from provincial and/or the federal government. Every taxpayer should know about the six basic steps of the tax-filing routine and how to identify them on the T1 General Tax Return, even if you use computer software to prepare your return:

Step 1 Identification and GST Credit Application
Step 2 Total Income Calculation (Up to Line 150)
Step 3 Net Income Calculation (Up to Line 236)
Step 4 Taxable Income Calculation (Includes Line 236 — Net Income — and finishes at Line 260)
Step 5 Non-Refundable Tax Credits (Up to Line 350)
Step 6 Refund or Balance Owing (either Line 484 or Line 485).

One of the most important lines on the return is the calculation of Net Income (Line 236). That is the figure upon which credits like the Goods and Services Tax Credit, the Child Tax Benefit, the Refundable Medical Expense Supplement and provincial tax credits are based.

20 FILE IN THE CORRECT PROVINCE OF RESIDENCE

Where were you on New Year's Eve? In Canada we file one tax return to compute federal taxes, and that same tax return is used to compute the provincial portion of taxes in all provinces except Quebec. (There, a separate provincial return is required.) You are taxed at the provincial tax rate of your province of residence as of December 31 of the tax year, and this is usually a percentage of basic federal tax. So, if a move is in your future, try to time it with a tax-wise eye. That is, move to a province with lower tax rates before year end, so that your entire year's income is taxed at this lower rate. If you are going to a province with a higher tax rate, try to move early in the new year to ensure adequate source deductions will be made.

21 ALWAYS FILE A TAX RETURN

Even if you do not have a taxable income, it pays to file a tax return. Lower-income earners who wish to receive refundable benefits, such as the Child Tax Benefit (CTB), the Goods and Services Tax Credit Prepayment (GSTC), or the Refundable Medical Expense Supplement, must file a tax return, as do residents of certain provinces that feature refundable tax credits.

Seniors who do not file income tax returns may not receive the right amount of Old Age Security. And investors may miss out on carrying forward important information such as RRSP Room, or capital loss balances. Others may miss carrying over unused deductions such as moving expenses, home office expenses, employment or business losses.

Remind any dependant you have who turned 19 during the year to file for his or her own GST Credit, or in some provinces, refundable provincial tax credits. Payments in the calendar year received for January through June will be based on income figures on the prior year, while the next fiscal period begins in July, based on information recorded on the current return. This credit is worth close to $200 (or more in the case of working singles), so it's well worth the tax-filing time.

22 ALWAYS PREPARE FAMILY TAX RETURNS TOGETHER

Tax filing should be a coordinated family event. To maximize your tax savings as a family unit, prepare family tax returns at the same time, starting with the lowest-income earner and finishing with the higher earner. You now have the required net and taxable income figures to maximize provisions such as the Spousal Amount, as well as transferable provisions such as the Age Amount, the $1,000 Pension Income Amount, the Tuition and Education Credits for full-time students and disabled dependants, medical expenses and RRSP transfers. You might even qualify as a family for refundable tax credits under both federal and provincial rules, including the Manitoba Learning Tax Credit, the new B.C. Family Bonus, and the Alberta Employment Tax Credits.

23 ALWAYS FILE ON TIME

Tardiness is expensive, especially if your return is filed late on purpose. It never makes sense to let Revenue Canada hang on to your tax refund. Further, if you filed late, thinking that you were owed a refund, but Revenue Canada later reassesses you and creates a balance due, interest and late filing penalties will be charged back to the original tax year.

By filing on time, midnight April 30 for most people, you can avoid a late filing penalty of 5% of the outstanding taxes due plus 1% per month of the outstanding balance for a maximum of 12 months. In addition, Revenue Canada will charge you interest on balances outstanding at what is known as the "prescribed rate" — the rate paid on treasury bills for the last quarter **plus** 4%. This can become very expensive.

Unincorporated small business owners and their spouses have until June 15 to file, but interest on any balance due is charged back to April 30. If Revenue Canada owes you a tax refund, no interest is paid to you until the return is filed and then only 45 days after the later of (1) the date the return is filed, or (2) the date the return was required to be filed.

24 DECLARE YOUR FOREIGN ASSETS

You can avoid some hefty penalties in the future if you are aware that you are required to report transfers and loans to a foreign trust, distributions from a foreign trust and any interests in foreign trusts with the return. Starting in 1998, taxpayers must begin reporting foreign investment properties worth more than $100,000. The value of funds or tangible property in foreign bank accounts, securities held outside Canada and shares of Canadian companies deposited with a foreign broker are amongst the assets that must be reported. The reporting of holdings in IRAs (Individual Retirement Accounts), shares in a non-resident corporation, interest in certain non-resident trusts, intangible property, and tangible property, such as commercial real estate, will also be caught. Specifically excluded from the proposed disclosure requirements is information about property used exclusively in an active business, personal use property (such as cottages, cars and boats), and property in an RRSP, RRIF, and a registered pension plan.

A special reporting form is also available for disclosure of foreign investment properties (T1135), foreign affiliates (T1134), transfers or loans to a foreign trust (T1141), and distributions from foreign trusts (T1142).

There are three types of exempt trusts: (1) a foreign retirement arrangement, (2) a trust establishing employee benefits under superannuation or retirement funds, or (3) a foreign mutual fund trust with at least 150 beneficiaries of the same units with certain fair market value requirements.

The government has stated that those who fail to disclose their foreign holdings could be subject to penalties of $500 a month for the first 24 months to a maximum of $12,000. After this an additional penalty of 10% will be levied.

✦ 25 TAX FILING CHANGES FOR NON-RESIDENTS

Sometimes non-residents, particularly former Canadian residents, continue to earn income in Canada. This can be from employment or self-employment in Canada or the selling of capital property held in Canada. Canada has tax treaties with over 60 countries, for the purpose of avoiding double taxation in these instances. Treaties either limit the rate of taxation applied to Canadian income sources earned by non-residents, or give exclusive taxing rights to one country or the other.

Certain rules have also been in place in cases where residency is difficult to determine, or where the taxpayer is a dual resident. Under a new interpretation announced with the February 24, 1998 budget, if a person is entitled, under a tax treaty, to non-resident status, this person will be deemed a non-resident under the Income Tax Act. This means this person will not be entitled to use any of the provisions of the Income Tax Act.

The only exception to this rule will be where a non-resident disposes of a Taxable Canadian Property, including Canadian real estate and certain Canadian shares. Income losses or capital gains in these instances will be considered to have arisen in Canada, unless the property is "treaty-protected," which means exempt from Canadian tax because of a treaty with another country.

26 FILE FOR THE NEW CCTB

The federal Child Tax Benefit (CTB) was revamped in the February 24, 1998 federal budget to become the Canada Child Tax Benefit (CCTB) after June 1998. This new initiative provides federal-provincial support for families through a National Child Benefit System. The two levels of government will adjust social assistance payments to take into account increases in the CCTB. The federal funding for this program will increase by $850 million annually.

As a result, filing a tax return will become one of the most significant financial events in the affairs of low-income families. This refundable credit is based on family net income and the number of children in the family. It is calculated automatically by Revenue Canada, based on information on the income tax return of the immediately prior year.

At the time of writing, besides the CCTB, complementary benefits, administered by Revenue Canada, were also available in several provinces:

- The BC Family Bonus and the BC Earned Income Benefit
- The Alberta Family Employment Tax Credit
- The Saskatchewan Child Benefit
- The New Brunswick Child Tax Benefit
- The Nova Scotia Child Benefit
- The Northwest Territories Child Benefit

These benefits will automatically stop the month after the child turns 18. There is no need to apply separately for the provincial/territorial credits; the information from the CCTB will be used.

27 KNOW HOW TO DECREASE NET INCOME TO INCREASE TAX CREDITS

You know that Net Income — Line 236 — influences the size of your Refundable Tax Credits. Net income is also the figure that is used in calculating numerous other tax provisions, including the amount of Old Age Security pension received, the amount of repayment, if any, required by Employment Insurance recipients, the Spousal Amount, the Equivalent-to-Spouse Amount, the claim for Additional Personal Amounts, medical expenses, and charitable donations. This figure is also used to compute certain provincial tax credits, some of which may be refundable, and provincial net income taxes.

By reducing your net income, you may receive more under each of these other tax provisions which, in the case of the Child Tax Benefits can affect your monthly cash flow. You'll also reduce any provincial net income taxes you may be subject to. (However, in the case of donations, a lower net income may restrict your claims.)

If you do nothing else, make sure you maximize the specific deductions available to reduce income in your individual circumstances.

28 SPECIFIC DEDUCTIONS AVAILABLE TO REDUCE YOUR NET INCOME

Which of the following tax deductions have you missed taking advantage of over the past several years?
- Registered Pension Plan Contributions
- RRSP Contributions
- Union/Professional Dues (Did you claim a GST/HST Rebate for any GST/HST charged on dues?)
- Child Care Expenses
- Attendant Care Expenses
- Business Investment Losses
- Moving Expenses
- Alimony or Separation Allowance paid in the year of separation or the immediately prior year, based on agreements in place before May 1, 1997 or in all cases, spousal support paid
- Carrying Charges, such as Safety Deposit Box fees, and interest on non-registered investments
- Exploration and Development Expenses
- Other Employment Expenses, such as auto expenses or home office costs
- Repayments of social benefits such as Employment Insurance Benefits or OAS.

P.S. Some less obvious deductions include the $500 exemption on scholarship or bursary income for students. Only the net amount, after the exemption, must be reported in income. So be sure to read the fine print for every line on the tax return.

29 REDUCE TAXABLE INCOME WITH CREATIVE DEDUCTIONS

Another group of deductions available on the tax return are rather obscure but can be lucrative. This is the specialized set of deductions used to arrive at taxable income, which is the figure on which federal tax is calculated. Check to see if you qualify to claim the following for the current or prior tax years:

- Employee Home Relocation Loan Deduction
- Stock Option and Shares Deduction
- Other Payments Deduction (for Workers' Compensation, Social Assistance or Federal Old Age Supplements added to income for the current tax year)
- Deduction for Non-Taxable Receipts of Foreign Pensions (such as German Pensions)
- Losses of Prior Years from Limited Partnerships
- Non-Capital Losses
- Capital Losses since 1972
- Capital Gains Deduction
- Northern Residents' Deduction
- Deduction for Child Support received from a U.S. resident or other income, such as pensions, tax exempt by virtue of a foreign tax treaty.

30 PRESERVE DEDUCTIONS LIKE THE RRSP

You may wish, at your discretion, to defer certain tax deductions for use in future years when your income is higher than it might be today. Planning to save RRSP room is a good example. Taxpayers can carry forward unused contribution room in their RRSP account as well as undeducted contributions.

For example, if you were eligible to contribute $5,000 in each of the years 1991 to 1996 for a total of $30,000, but could only afford to contribute $1,000 each year, you would have $24,000 in unused contribution room to carry forward and use on the 1998 return. The contribution must actually be made to be deductible, either during the year or in the first 60 days of the new year. Starting in 1996, RRSP room can be carried forward indefinitely.

By planning wisely, you can use that room to offset a year of high income — perhaps when you dispose of a capital property, or receive a bonus. That's the time the unused RRSP contribution room of prior years can be used to reduce significantly — or even eliminate — the amount of tax that is payable on these unusual transactions.

Lower earners who are taxable should also consder making an RRSP contribution, if they have RRSP "room." The resulting lower net income might create higher Refundable Medical Expense Supplements, Child Tax Benefits, GST Credits, or other deductions or credits.

31 LEARN TO PLAY THE GAME WITH REVENUE CANADA

Someone once said that the relationship a taxpayer has with Revenue Canada is not unlike that of two teams in a football game. Both are trying to control the football and score points. There are, however, a couple of real differences in playing ball with Revenue Canada.

First, instead of a football, you are playing with your own money. This can put an entirely different "spin" on your positioning. Second, you are playing a game with an opponent who is also the referee and knows all of the rules, plus a few others that are not published information. You may work very hard, but without an even playing field your odds of getting that football — your money — into the end zone (that is, into your own pocket) are not that good...unless, of course, you too know the rules.

The moral of this tip? Know how Revenue Canada plays ball, especially when you are down a few points. (Or, if tax training camp doesn't suit you, hire some talent to help you score some financial touchdowns.)

32 REQUEST THAT INTEREST AND PENALTIES BE WAIVED IN SEVERE HARDSHIP CASES

If circumstances beyond your control — a serious accident or illness, serious emotional or mental distress, including a death in the family, or a natural or man-made disaster — caused you to miss making a tax payment when due, Revenue Canada can waive the penalty and interest charges that would otherwise be imposed under the law for failure to file or to pay.

The same new rule applies if the penalties or interest resulted from erroneous actions at the tax department, such as processing delays that caused you not to be informed in a reasonable time period of an amount that was owing, errors in written matters, incorrect advice on instalment remittance billings, or errors in processing the information on your return.

You can request that interest and penalties be cancelled or waived in such cases by making a written submission to the tax department, outlining the facts and reasons for your position that the events were out of your control.

This tip can save you thousands of dollars, if Revenue Canada agrees with your position.

33 MINIMIZE EXPOSURE TO REVENUE CANADA CHARGES

You already know that by filing on time, midnight April 30, you can avoid a late filing penalty of 5% of the outstanding taxes due plus 1% per month of the outstanding balance for a maximum of 12 months. The filing deadline has been extended to June 15 for unincorporated small businesses, but an interest charge still applies from May 1 on if you owe money to Revenue Canada.

Interest charges can also be avoided on balances resulting from deficient quarterly instalments, or gross negligence penalties which, by the way, can be avoided entirely if you tell Revenue Canada about under-reported income or overstated expenses before they find out. Voluntary compliance can reduce your tax audit costs significantly. So, if you have a guilty conscience, request an adjustment to prior-filed returns to correct any erroneous filing. It can pay off handsomely to have a spotless filing record with Revenue Canada.

34 KEEP YOUR WELL-ORGANIZED TAX RECORDS FOR AT LEAST SIX YEARS

Probably the most difficult part of filing a tax return is gathering all the information to outline the past year of your life. All most employees must do is wait for their T4 slips to arrive; others look to their mailbox for T5s (investment income summaries) or various pension income amounts.

If you are self-employed, a commission salesperson or an investor, some transactions are self-reported. The onus of proof for all figures on the tax return rests with you. Always file a return with one thought in mind: Will these documents and figures pass a tax audit?

The answer to that question depends largely on how well you'll remember the justification for your claims two or three years from now when the auditor may call on you. Keep meticulous notes in your working papers.

Keep logs and journals of your business travels or the number of clients you see in your home office. When you entertain, write the name of your client or associate on the back of the chit, as well as the purpose of the meeting. Keep your records for a minimum of six years from the end of the calendar year in which you received your Notice of Assessment.

⬟ 35 USE CARRY-OVER OPPORTUNITIES

You can take certain unused tax deductions or credits incurred in one year and use them to offset income or taxes in another year. This can mean recovery of prior-paid taxes or the reduction of future tax liabilities. Check your old tax returns for the following provisions:

1. *Home office expenses:* these cannot be used to increase or create a loss from employment or self-employment. Unused claims can be carried forward and applied next year.
2. *Unused donations* can be carried forward for a five-year period.
3. *Moving expenses* can be carried forward if expenses exceed income earned at the new location.
4. *Unused tuition/education credits* from prior years can be used on the student's return.
5. *A Capital Cost Allowance Claim* for those with small businesses, farms or rental properties may be claimed to the taxpayer's advantage.
6. *An Alternative Minimum Tax Amount* paid in a prior year may be used to reduce taxes and surtaxes this year.

Other important information to be carried forward from this year:

7. Unused business investment losses.
8. Unused non-capital losses of prior years.
9. Unused capital losses of prior years.
10. Unused Capital Gains Deduction room of prior years for the purposes of the $500,000 Super Exemption still available to owners of Small Business Corporation Shares or Qualifying Farm Properties. (Use Form T657 to make this claim.)
11. Cumulative Net Investment Losses.
12. Unused RRSP contribution room.
13. Unclaimed RRSP contributions.
14. Unclaimed past service contributions under an RPP (Registered Pension Plan).

15. The amount of your Capital Gains Election and the new Adjusted Cost Base of your assets, including the exempt gains balances available for mutual funds or eligible capital property on which an election was made.
16. Fair Market Value (FMV) of assets acquired by gift, transfer or inheritance.
17. Any unused amounts of a student's tuition/education tax credits, or unclaimed student loan interest.

Upon request, Revenue Canada can also update you on their records of certain balances, like your capital and non-capital loss balances, or unclaimed home office expenses. To be sure, however, it is best to keep these records on statements filed with your personal tax records, and to review last year's carry-over balances.

Also, be sure to instruct the executor of your estate or other trusted assistants about these carry-over balances, so they have the information should you become incapacitated. Because such events are normally unforeseen, a highly organized tax portfolio will make life easier for those who act on your behalf, and could save you and your family thousands of dollars.

36 BREAK THE TASK DOWN

Start early in the year to prepare your family's taxes, and then use a three-step process to finish the task.

Step one: gather and separate all information about each family member, including birthdates, Social Insurance Numbers, and source documents for income and deductions. Make sure you have a tax return and the appropriate tax guide for each provision. Separate the T-slips and sort copies for submission to Revenue Canada. Obtain any auxiliary tax forms for deductions such as child care expenses from the government before you start to compute your taxes. Or use a computer tax program for this purpose.*

Step two is to enter the data and begin the number crunching.

Step three, which should be done after a break away from this work, is the checking and assembly of the tax return for mailing or electronic filing.

---

*If you have recently acquired a computer, you may also wish to try preparing your taxes using one of the many excellent software packages available. This is a great way to take control of the amount of tax you pay, and to do some tax planning throughout the year. Plus, the program does the tax calculations for you automatically...a real bonus!

3

PLAN FOR FAMILY TAX SAVINGS

Do you know...

* *Maximizing your available tax deductions can reduce your net income...*
* *Lower net family incomes can reap higher federal and provincial credits...*
* *There are ample opportunities to reduce tax by splitting income within the family...*
* *The tax system offers opportunities for saving for a child's education...*

Tax assistance for those who live with a family comes in a variety of formats in Canada. The taxpayer may claim deductions that reduce taxable income, non-refundable tax credits that are used to reduce the actual taxes paid, and tax-free refundable tax credits that are sent to certain Canadians, whose incomes fall under certain pre-set thresholds.

The most lucrative of these provisions is the tax-free Canada Child Tax Benefit. Every three months Revenue Canada distributes approximately $450 million dollars in Child Tax Benefits to over three million families across Canada. Starting in 1998, certain provincial Child Tax Benefits will also be administered and distributed by Revenue Canada.

The CTB can only be received if a tax return is filed by both parents of a child, because the amount received is based on net family income. Therefore, filing a tax return can really pay off. But the trick is to make sure you get the most from these available credits. This means watching your net income size (Line 236).

To reduce your net income, the next step in the chain of provisions available to families includes the claiming of child care expenses and RRSP deductions, as well as child support payments for certain taxpayers who signed agreements with their ex-spouses before May 1, 1997.

Finally, it is important to work with the available non-refundable tax credits for the Basic Personal Amount, the new Personal Amount Supplement, the Spousal or Equivalent-to-Spouse Amounts, Amounts for Infirm Dependants, the new Caregivers' Amount, Disability Amount, Tuition and Education Amounts, including the new Student Loan Interest Amount, medical expenses, and charitable donations.

The key to maximizing your tax-free benefits from the government is to use all applicable tax deductions to reduce your net income and your taxes payable. Next, claim all the Non-Refundable Tax Credits you are entitled to. Then, transferrable tax deductions and credits can be used to reduce the tax liability of supporting persons.

In addition it is important to do some basic investment planning, to use every opportunity to have lower-income earners generate the investment earnings both inside and outside an RRSP. To do so, however, it is necessary to know how to avoid Revenue Canada's Attribution Rules. These concepts are discussed below.

By filing tax returns as a unit, rather than as individuals, it is possible to reduce the family tax burden. Remember, start with the lowest-income earner and work your way up.

37 FILE TO RECEIVE THE MONTHLY CHILD TAX BENEFIT

You can stop looking. There are a number of provisions relating to the expenses of raising a child on the tax form, but there is no place to actually "claim" a separate amount for a dependant under the age of 19.

You will want to apply for the Canada Child Tax Benefit, though. This is a "refundable" tax credit. The lower your family net income the better the chances of receiving full credits. To receive it? Simply file a tax return. In fact, the Child Tax Benefit, a lucrative monthly payment to Canadian families, can only be received if *both spouses* file a tax return every year.

The Child Tax Benefit payment for your children is therefore determined through the size of the "family net income." The parent and the qualified dependant must reside together in the same home in Canada; therefore non-resident dependants will not qualify.

If the child resides with two parents in two different locations concurrently, only one parent can be eligible in any given month to receive the benefits. In that case, the primary caregiver must be identified. This is determined by specifics on who gives the most details of care. The person who is "eligible" — that is, qualified by the net family income as per the income tax return — receives the CCTB.

If the child leaves one parent's home to live with another, the second parent becomes eligible for the credit in the month the dependant starts living with him/her. If the dependant leaves the home for a temporary absence (i.e., holiday, school, work, medical care), the parent still qualifies to receive the benefits throughout the child's temporary period of absence.

The CCTB will not be computed at all if neither parent files a tax return. Or, where only one person files, the CCTB will be advanced to you for a while, "with warnings." Then repayment is demanded should your spouse fail to file — another compelling reason to invest, rather than spend, this particular government cheque!

38 THE NEWLY ENHANCED NATIONAL CHILD BENEFITS SYSTEM

Revenue Canada calculates the new National Child Benefits based on the number of children under 19 entered on the tax return, the family net income, the family "working income," and the child care expense deductions claimed. Under the federal CCTB, the following maximum amounts are available: a basic benefit of $1,020* ($85 a month) for each child under age 19; a supplement of $75 ($6.25 a month) for the third and each additional child; and a further supplement of $213 ($17.75 a month) for each child under age seven. (However, this latter amount is reduced by 25% of any child care amount claimed on the tax return.)

There's more: the Family Working Supplement for low-income earners provides for an additional per-child amount to low-income families. This amounts to $605 for the first child, $405 for the second and $330 for the third and subsequent children. Reductions in the supplement will apply at certain income levels. (See later Tax Tips.)

"Working income" is defined as income from employment, self-employment, training allowances or scholarships, and disability payments

---

*Note: The figures will change in Alberta and Quebec. As mentioned previously, Revenue Canada now administers Child Tax Benefits on behalf of several provinces.

under the Canada Pension Plan. (Capital gains resulting from foreclosures or repossessions under conditional sales contracts are excluded from this definition.)

As you can see, the computation of the amount of benefits you may be entitled to is complex, but the important thing to remember is that the size of your family net income, your marital status and the number of children you have, all will affect your monthly Child Tax Benefit. For these reasons, a visit to your tax professional before you begin a conjugal relationship can help you determine how your monthly income will be affected by this decision. It can also really pay to reduce your family net income with RRSPs and other legitimate tax deductions in an attempt to qualify for or increase a Child Tax Benefit (CTB) payment.

39 TAKE THE TIME TO CALCULATE THE TAX-FREE SAVINGS POTENTIAL

Once you receive your CTB eligibility statement from Revenue Canada, take the time to calculate the potential tax-free accumulations you can save for your child's university, first house, car, etc. with the CTB working for you. Take our common-law couple, Jody and Mark, as an example.

Each earns $12,000 annually at their respective jobs. Filing a tax return could reap CTBs of about $125 each month for their baby, Angie, assuming no child care expenses are claimed. That amounts to about $1,500 each year until the child turns 7, if all things remain equal. From age 7 to 18, the monthly amount drops to about $100 a month or $1,200 a year. If this is saved faithfully (and all other factors relating to income and number of children remain the same), a fund well over $20,000 plus earnings could be accumulated by the child in 18 years. All earnings would be taxed in her hands, provided the amounts were deposited to a separate account used only for CTB deposits. What a way to split income and send Angie off — virtually tax-free — on the road to success!

Note: With recent enhancements under the new National Child Benefit System, tax-free provincial child tax benefits received can also be invested in the name of the child to add to the accumulated education fund.

40 THE PERSONAL AMOUNT SUPPLEMENT

A broad-based tax decrease will apply **in** 1998 and future years to low- and middle-income earners. The Supplement will provide an additional "non-refundable" credit of up to $500, for taxpayers who are single with no dependants, and an additional $500 in cases where a Spousal or Equivalent-to-Spouse claim is available.

However, for tax year 1998, only one-half the supplement will be allowed, so that the above amounts are limited to a $250 maximum. The Supplement will be reduced by 4% of net income in excess of $6,956.

Example: Bob is single, 25 years old, and has no dependants. He had net income in 1998 of $15,000.

Basic Supplement		$500 (a)
Reduction of Supplement		
Net Income	$15,000	
Less	$ 6,956	
	$ 8,044 × 4% = $322 (b)	
Total Supplement (a-b)		$178 **1/2 for 1998 = $89**

41 THE TAX-FREE ZONE INCREASES FOR SOME

The Supplementary Basic Personal Amount has the effect of increasing the "Tax-Free Zone" to $6706 for some taxpayers in 1998, and $6956 for 1999. These thresholds will be used to calculate the following provisions found elsewhere on the tax return:

- amount of CCA claimed on small business returns
- amount of RRSP contribution claimed/carried forward
- amount of Business Investment Losses claimed/carried forward
- CCA claims on employment expenses on Line 229
- amount of capital/non-capital losses claimed/carried forward
- Disability Amount claimable/transferrable
- Tuition/education Amounts claimable/carried forward/transferable
- Student Loan Interest Amount claimable/carried forward
- Amounts Transferred to Spouse
- Medical Expenses claimable/carried forward
- Donations and Gifts claimable/carried forward
- Investment tax credit claimable/carried forward
- Labour-sponsored funds tax credit claimable/carried forward

Some careful tax planning will be required to take into account these new rules, which will affect low-income earners in your family.

42 KNOW THE DEFINITION OF A SPOUSE FOR TAX PURPOSES

You may be able to claim the Spousal Amount of up to $5,380 if you live with someone of the opposite sex to whom you are legally married.

If you are living in a common-law relationship with someone of the opposite sex, that person will be considered your spouse for income tax purposes if you lived together in one of two circumstances. First, if you lived together on December 31 and that person is the parent of your child (naturally or adoptive), you are considered spouses for tax purposes, regardless of how long you've lived together. Second, if you don't have a child together, the spousal status exists if you have lived with that person in a conjugal relationship for a period of 12 months ending in the tax year, or for a continuous 12-month period sometime in the past. When this 12-month period is calculated, include any period of separation less than 90 days.

If you meet these qualifications, you can claim your common-law spouse for the "Spousal Amount" and take advantage of all other transferable provisions available to married couples through the tax system.

However, reporting common-law living arrangements could reduce or eliminate their GST Credit and certain provincial tax credits otherwise available if the couple lived apart. This is because these claims would now be based on their combined net family income.

43 IN LOVE AND IN WAR, TIMING CAN MAKE THE DIFFERENCE

In the year of marriage, the spouse's net income for the whole year is used for the purposes of determining tax credits and deductions. If the net income of your new spouse is low now, and if that spouse expects to earn more next year, consider planning the marriage before the end of the current tax year to create a Spousal Amount on your tax return sooner. The tax savings might finance at least a part of the honeymoon!

On the other hand, there may be tax advantages to postponing the wedding where there are children in the family unit who are not the product of a union with your spouse-to-be. In that case, you'll be considered single if you and your common-law spouse have not lived together for at least one year in the current year or sometime in the past. This means that you can preserve an Equivalent-to-Spouse Amount for your child at least for this tax year.

Because the size of the Spousal Amount you can claim is dependent upon your spouse's net income, you should be able to reduce net income size with certain allowable tax deductions such as the RRSP or the Child Care Expense deduction.

44 CLAIM THE EQUIVALENT-TO-SPOUSE AMOUNT IF YOU'RE A SINGLE PARENT

A single person, or someone who is divorced, separated or widowed will qualify to claim the Equivalent-to-Spouse Amount for a dependent child who is under 18 and with whom s/he lived during the year. The claim is also extended to those singles who supported a dependent parent or grandparent, or a relative over 18 who is mentally or physically infirm.

The claim is lucrative; it is calculated the same way as the Spousal Amount. That means that if the dependant had a net income of less than $538, the full claim of $5,380 is allowed. That calculates out to an actual federal-provincial tax saving of about $1,500, depending on your provincial tax rate. There are more savings, through an enhanced GST Credit and various provincial tax provisions, aimed at recognizing the dependant's Equivalent-to-Spouse status.

A reduced claim will result if the dependant's net income is over $538 but less than $5,918.

For unmarried parents of the same child who live together in a common-law relationship, the Equivalent-to-Spouse Amount for the child is denied. Possible tax relief can be obtained by claiming the Spousal Amount elsewhere in the tax return for the common-law spouse, depending on that person's net income.

If you and your spouse were separated but then reconciled during the year, you can choose to claim the Spousal Amount or the Equivalent-to-Spouse. This is a new provision for tax years after 1996.

45 CLAIM DEPENDANTS OVER 18 WHO ARE INFIRM

If you support a person over the age of 18 who is mentally or physically infirm, you will qualify for a special non-refundable tax credit claim on your tax return. It is not necessary for the dependant to be so severely incapacitated that daily living activities are markedly restricted. However, the disability must restrict the dependant from being self-supporting. Persons over the age of 65 are generally considered to be claimable by virtue of their age and infirmity. Net income of the dependant will be a restricting factor in making this claim.

Even if you are claiming this special amount for dependants over 18 who are infirm, be sure also to file a tax return individually for these dependants to tap into their rightful GST Credit.

In 1998 the maximum tax credit is $2,353, and the dependant can have a net income of $4,103 before the credit is reduced.

 # 46 THE CAREGIVERS' TAX CREDIT

For the 1998 and subsequent tax years, a new non-refundable tax credit will be available for individuals who provide in-home care to parents or grandparents who are 65 years of age or older.

This credit will also apply if the in-home care is provided for the individual's child, grandchild, parent, grandparent, sibling, uncle, aunt, niece or nephew or if the person is an adult who is dependent on the individual due to a physical or mental infirmity, and is at least 18 years of age.

The maximum amount of this new credit is $2,353. This will be received in full if the dependant's net income does not exceed $11,500. If the dependant's net income is more than $11,500 but less than $13,853, then the credit will be reduced by 17% of the amount by which the dependant's net income exceeds $11,500.

No credit will be available if the dependant's net income exceeds $13,853, or if the Credit for Infirm Dependants Over 18 has been claimed in respect of that dependant by any person.

47 TRANSFER TAX CREDITS FROM ONE SPOUSE TO ANOTHER

Spouses, including common-law spouses, should always prepare their taxes simultaneously. The lower earner's return is prepared first and, as mentioned, that person should file for the GST Credit for the family to create income "in his or her own right."

Once this return is completed you can quickly identify whether the spouse's net income is too high for a claim under the Spousal Amount. To be considered: will an RRSP contribution bring about a non-taxable status? Does the spouse have RRSP contribution room: if so, is there still time for the spouse to contribute? (RRSP contributions must be made during the year or within the first 60 days of the year end.) Is there a better benefit if the higher earner contributes to the RRSP? In 1998 the spouse may earn as much as $6,706 before income becomes taxable. This is thanks to the new Personal Amount Supplement.

If the spouse is not taxable, determine whether the higher-income earner can transfer any available age amount, pension income amount, tuition or education amount or disability amount to his or her own return. Find out by completing a Revenue Canada Schedule 2.

If the lower earner is taxable, consider claiming medical expenses on that person's return. This could increase the family tax refund, because medical expenses are reduced by 3% of net income. Then the new Refundable Medical Expense Supplement is calculated. Spouses considered to be agents of each other for the purposes of the medical expenses, charitable donations or political contributions made by either, so group and claim them to the family's best tax benefit.

48 USE REVENUE CANADA'S ATTRIBUTION RULES TO YOUR ADVANTAGE

Earnings generated from principal that was transferred from a high-income earner to the spouse or a minor will generally be taxed in the hands of the transferor. This is true of interest, dividends or capital gains income earned on money transferred to your spouse, or interest and dividends earned on money transferred to your minor child.

For example, if you give your spouse $5,000 to invest in a Canada Savings Bond, the resulting interest is taxed back in your hands. You can avoid these rules if you can establish that the income should be properly attributed to the spouse, who had income "in his or her own right."

Income "earned in your own right" includes income from your own employment or self-employment, inheritances received, or income tax refunds or credits such as the Child Tax Benefit or Goods and Services Tax Credit. So, rather than spend that monthly Child Tax Benefit, have the lower-income earner invest it. The resulting investment earnings will be taxed in the lower earner's hands.

49 SPLIT FUTURE PENSION INCOME: BUY AN RRSP IN THE NAME OF YOUR SPOUSE

Looking down the road a bit, perhaps you are aware that your spouse will not have the same level of taxable pension income when you both retire. Your family unit ultimately pays more tax in this case because the majority of pension accumulations are in the hands of one spouse, who probably is in a higher tax bracket than the other spouse.

Plan to split RRSP accumulations in retirement by depositing your RRSP contribution in the name of your spouse, to balance out accumulations in each person's hands. You'll get the tax deduction, but your lower-earning spouse will be taxed on subsequent withdrawals, provided the money stays in the plan at least three years from the date of the last spousal RRSP contribution.

50 NO SPOUSE? BUY AN RRSP FOR YOUR CHILD

If you are a single parent, you can provide your child with the money to buy an RRSP, which shelters the earnings within the plan from the tax man until the amounts are withdrawn. As the child will not likely withdraw the amounts before age 18, resulting earnings are taxable in the child's hands. There is a catch here: the child must have "earned income" in the immediate prior year, or unused RRSP contribution room to qualify to make RRSP contributions. So, if your child has a part-time job, babysits or has a paper route, always be sure to file a tax return for him or her to create the necessary RRSP contribution room, especially since unused RRSP room can now be carried forward indefinitely. The child may not contribute any amount above the RRSP Contribution Room limit, which is currently $2,000.

51 FILE A TAX RETURN FOR TEENAGERS

Always file a tax return for any family member who is earning a part-time income from employment or self-employment. Take 13-year-old Shannon, for example, who last year earned $50 each week looking after the neighbours' children after school. This translates into $2,500 after 50 weeks of work, and 18% of this amount qualifies for contribution to Shannon's RRSP. That's $450.

Why would you want to calculate this figure if she is not taxable and the RRSP contribution is not needed?

It's simple: If Shannon earns the same income every year for five years until she turns 18, she will have accumulated $2,250 in unused RRSP contribution room. To register this amount of "room" with Revenue Canada, she must have filed a tax return for every year — in this case as a self-employed child caregiver. (She may also qualify for some lucrative deductions.)

At age 19, Shannon finds a full-time job and earns $18,000. She can now make an RRSP contribution of $2,250, which will save her approximately 28% (depending upon which province she lives in) or $630 in taxes. Very worthwhile indeed.

52 LOAN YOUR SPOUSE OR CHILD MONEY TO MAKE AN INVESTMENT

You can make a loan to your spouse or minor child to make an interest or dividend-bearing investment with the resulting earnings taxed to that spouse or child, if you follow the proper procedures. That is, a loan that bears a commercial rate of interest — calculated, charged and actually paid each year within 30 days of year end — is considered "legitimate," and resulting earnings are taxed in the spouse's or child's hands. Be sure also to provide for repayment terms.

Remember, the key to income splitting is to have the lower earners in the family invest, rather than spend, their income.

53 REINVEST SECOND-GENERATION EARNINGS

Earnings generated by investment income that was previously attributed is taxed to the lower-income earner. For example, if a father gave his daughter $10,000 to invest in a Guaranteed Investment Certificate, the resulting earnings would be taxed to him. However, if the interest earnings themselves were reinvested by the daughter in another investment (perhaps a Canada Savings Bond), the offsetting income from that second investment would be properly taxed to the daughter. This is called "second-generation earnings."

54 BUY A BUSINESS FOR YOUR SPOUSE OR CHILD

Business income earned from dollars or property transferred from the higher earner to the spouse or minor child is exempt from the attribution rules. This means the spouse or child may earn, and be taxed upon, the profits of the company. However, in the case of a spouse only, the profits on the sale of capital assets acquired directly from the higher-income earner would be attributed back to the higher-income earner.

55 GIVE A GIFT — TAX-FREE

Feel free to give to your minor child or grandchild, niece or nephew or other child with whom you are related or dealing "at arm's length." Only interest and dividend earnings that result from your gift are taxed back to you.

There are no tax consequences if the child spends the money on consumer goods, pays for education or acquires a tax exempt principal residence, or a capital asset, such as a mutual fund that will result in a capital gain.

56 BUY CAPITAL ASSETS IN THE NAME OF YOUR CHILD OR GRANDCHILD

Yes, you read correctly. You can avoid the Attribution Rules by giving your minor child or grandchild a capital asset, such as a capital stock or mutual fund. The profit on the sale of the asset, or capital gain, is attributed to the child. Resulting capital gains will likely be taxed at a much lower tax rate in the hands of the child, if at all. On subsequent dispositions, be sure to take into account any Capital Gains Elections made on behalf of the child's accrued asset valuations in his or her 1994 tax return.

Unfortunately, dividends or "other income" earned on the capital stock gifted to a minor child are attributed back to the donor.

57 SAY ADIEU IN TAX HARMONY

You have learned that when you marry during the tax year, the Spousal Amount is based on net income for the entire year. If you separate or become divorced, however, use only the net income of your spouse up to date of separation. A Spousal Amount and/or a Personal Amount Supplement could result, making a good argument for separating in the early months of the tax year. But, should you reconcile and live together again before year end, Revenue Canada will consider you to be married for the whole year, in which case the spouse's net income for the whole year must again be used.

Common-law spouses who break up are subject to a "90-day rule." If, for example, you separated 90 days or more into the year, you are not considered to be "spouses" anymore for the purposes of the Income Tax Act. But, if you reconcile before year end, you are considered "spouses" again, with all of the relevant tax provisions intact, if you previously cohabited for a full 12-month period, or have a natural or adoptive child.

Justifying your Spousal Amount claims could therefore be a challenge. If your personal life is that complicated, consider keeping a detailed documentation in a "relationship log"!

58 CERTAIN SUPPORT PAYMENTS ARE TAX DEDUCTIBLE TO THE PAYOR

If you are considering a separation or divorce, there is important planning news regarding the taxation of *support payments* for children and spouse on new agreements made after May 1, 1997: *child support payments* will no longer be taxable to the recipient or deductible by the payor, but *spousal support payments* will still be considered taxable to the recipient and tax deductible to the payor.

If you decide to keep the old agreement, signed before May 1, 1997, in place, amounts paid for the support of the spouse or children of a failed union depended upon the existence of all the following circumstances:

1. Amounts must be paid for the maintenance of the spouse or children, or both on a periodic basis.
2. The spouses must be living apart at the time the payments were made and throughout the remainder of the year.
3. The parties must be separated and amounts paid pursuant to a divorce, judicial separation or written separation agreement.
4. Amounts are deductible if paid in the year or the immediately preceding year. (In the latter case, adjust the prior-filed return.)

To change to the new system, both parents jointly elect to have old agreements cease to apply as of an agreed-upon date on or after May 1, 1997 (file Form T1157). The new rules will automatically apply if:

1. The amount of child support is changed by a court order or agreement made on or after May 1, 1997 (file Form T1158), or
2. The court order specifically says the new tax rules will apply to payments on or after May 1, 1997.

You may wish to reconsider old arrangements in light of enhanced new Canada Child Tax Benefits. (See Tip 61.)

59 LEGAL FEES IN FAMILY DISPUTES MAY BE TAX DEDUCTIBLE

While the costs of obtaining a divorce or separation are not tax deductible, any amounts expended on legal fees to enforce the payment of previously established financial commitments are allowed, if the amounts were taxable to the recipient.

If in the various legal proceedings the court orders the recipient to make a repayment of separation allowances previously received, the amounts so repaid are tax deductible in the current year and either of the two following years, if the amounts were previously taxable.

60 TAXABLE ALIMONY/MAINTENANCE INCOME QUALIFIES FOR RRSP PURPOSES

The recipient of taxable child support or spousal support payments is required to add them to income and pay tax at the applicable marginal tax rate. Here is some bad news: this income may necessitate the payment of quarterly tax instalments to Revenue Canada to avoid interest charges. You may be able to reduce or avoid these instalments entirely if you make a contribution to an RRSP. Taxable alimony/maintenance payments received in the immediately prior year will create RRSP contribution room which will reduce the amount of tax you pay on this income.

The payor of these taxable support amounts, incidentally, must reduce his or her RRSP earned income for RRSP purposes by the amount of the Alimony/Maintenance deduction taken.

If you are now receiving tax-free Child Support, your RRSP contribution in future years will be reduced, while those who lost their Child Support deduction through these tax changes can take comfort in the fact that their RRSP Room will generally increase.

61 NEW CHILD TAX BENEFITS MAY BE CAUSE FOR SUPPORT RECLASSIFICATION

Under the new national child benefits program, in which provincial child benefit programs are available to complement the federal programs, it may be to your advantage to take a fresh look at your old pre-May 1997 child support agreement.

Under those old agreements, amounts paid remained taxable to the recipient and tax deductible to the payor. However, it may now be worthwhile to consider an election to have the payments treated as non-taxable and non-deductible, under new May 1 rules. The elimination of the child support from the net income of the recipient could create supplementary monthly benefits by way of the Canada Child Tax Benefits.

Besides the CCTB, complementary benefits, administered by Revenue Canada, are now also available in the following provinces:

- The BC Family Bonus and the BC Earned Income Benefit
- The Alberta Family Employment Tax Credit
- The Saskatchewan Child Benefit
- The New Brunswick Child Tax Benefit
- The Nova Scotia Child Benefit and
- The Northwest Territories Child Benefit

Therefore, particularly if both parties are in the lowest tax brackets, a switch to non-taxable, non-deductible status of the child support payments could reap higher overall benefits to the family due to the distribution of enhanced tax-free refundable tax credits. Do the numbers both ways to be sure.

62 SPOUSAL SUPPORT PLANNING CAN BE PROFITABLE

As mentioned, payments made for spousal support in agreements negotiated after April 30, 1997 will continue to be taxable to the recipient and deductible to the payor.

In cases where the recipient has little or no income, it may be an idea to structure the agreement to receive taxable spousal support of at least $6,456 (the Basic Personal Amount) plus any Personal Amount Supplement the recipient is entitled to, and any RRSP contribution room available to keep the receipts tax-free. The balance of the payments, if any, could be structured as tax-free child support after April 30, 1997.

 ## 63 MAKE RESIDENCE MOVES TAX EFFICIENT

A relationship breakdown could precede a family move. If you are looking at such a circumstance, there are numerous tax-planning options to be aware of.

First, Canadians are taxed at their province of residence as at December 31 of the tax year. So, if you are considering a move to a province that has higher tax rates than the one you currently live in, plan the move early in the next year, if possible. If you move before year end, your income from the whole year will be taxed at the new province's rate, which will usually result in a tax liability at year end because those rates will not be reflected in your employer's remittance requirements.

The opposite is true if you are moving to a province with lower tax rates. Try to make this move before year end so that all of your income for the year is taxed at those lower tax rates.

You should be aware that numerous provinces have recently dropped their provincial tax rates, including New Brunswick, Quebec, Ontario, Manitoba, Saskatchewan, Alberta and BC. Make sure you keep abreast of your tax advantages before you move.

 ## 64 MOVING EXPENSE DEDUCTIONS ARE LUCRATIVE

The tax deduction for moving expenses can be lucrative if you moved to start a job, a business or go to post-secondary school full-time at the new location.

Save all receipts pertaining to the move, including real estate commissions paid on the sale of your old residence and removal expenses, costs of meals and lodging en route and up to 15 days' temporary living accommodations in the new location, all provided you moved at least 40 kilometres closer to a new work location from your old metropolitan area. (This 40 kilometres is measured as the distance between the new work location and the old, using the shortest possible normal route of travel.)

New deductible moving expenses for 1998 include the costs of maintaining a vacant former residence, such as mortgage interest and property taxes. The deductibility of these expenses will be limited to the least of three amounts:

1. the actual amount of maintenance expenses
2. the portion of those expenses attributable to a period of three months
3. $5,000

In addition, numerous incidental expenses, such as the cost of changing the address on legal documents, replacing driver's licenses and utility hook-ups/disconnections will now be deductible.

 ## 65 RESP SAVINGS OPPORTUNITIES INCREASE

If you are looking for ways to shelter savings for your child's education, you may wish to look into the merits of a Registered Educational Savings Plan. Starting in 1997, the annual limit on the amount of total contributions to a RESP for each beneficiary increased to the lesser of $4,000 per year to a lifetime maximum of $42,000 per student. And starting in 1998, the government will help you finance your child's education with a new Canada Education Savings Grant.

While contributions made to a RESP have no tax consequences for the contributor (i.e., the amounts are not tax deductible), the accumulations of earnings on the investment (including the CESG) are not taxed until distribution to the student in the future. At that time, the earnings are reported by the student as an "educational assistance payment."

Because these increased RESP contribution limits may eventually serve to increase the student's income in the future, tax returns should be filed by all young persons with part-time earnings. This is to build up RRSP contribution room, which can be used to offset the student's taxable income in the future.

Starting in 1998, should the student decide not to go to post-secondary school, RESP income may be returned to the contributor if the amounts have accumulated in the plan for at least 10 years. Such withdrawals will be reported as income, unless the contributor has RRSP contribution room, in which case up to $40,000 in tax-sheltered income accumulations may be transferred to the RRSP ($50,000 starting in 1999). If RESP income is not fully offset by RRSP deductions, a penalty tax of 20% will apply to the unsheltered RESP income.

66 THE CANADA EDUCATION SAVINGS GRANT

Beginning in 1998, the federal government will provide a CESG of up to 20% of the first $2,000 contributed to a RESP, to a maximum of $400 per year per child. The CESG will be paid directly into the RESP set up by the contributor.

Every child under 18 years of age will be able to accumulate CESG contribution room of $2,000 per year. Therefore, in situations where RESP contributions may not have been made for a few years, the 20% grant will be paid in a subsequent year in which RESP contributions are made, based on cumulative room, or the amount of RESP contributions in the year up to $4,000, whichever is less.

It is also noteworthy that starting in 1998, RESP contributions for a child aged 16 or 17 will be eligible for the grant only if there have been contributions of at least $100 annually made for the child in any 4 years before the year in which the child turned 16, or if the total previous contributions were at least $4,000 in the year before the child turned 16.

If a child decides to forego pursuing higher education, the CESG must be returned to the government by the RESP, although the earnings generated by the grant may be retained within the plan. The contributor has the option of naming another beneficiary or withdrawing the balance of the funds. Such withdrawals must be included in income and are subject to an additional 20% penalty tax, unless the amounts are transferred into the contributor's RRSP. (RRSP room must be available.)

Note: It is important that a Social Insurance Number is obtained for each child, as the Canada Education Savings Grants will not be paid out without one.

67 THINK AHEAD

You should always have your family's financial legacy in mind when you prepare income tax returns. Are your assets protected if something should happen to you? How will the transfer of the cottage, your business, or other assets be affected by tax rules if you die? Will your child still be able to go to college? Will your spouse know how to invest your money or where your safety deposit box is?

Proper tax planning includes a review of all of these tax questions, a review of your will, a review of your tax-free life insurance policy benefit provisions, and a review of your wishes and concerns. Tax filing time is a great time to update this process, once your return is safely "put to bed" for another year.

CHAPTER 4

TAX-WISE TIPS FOR STUDENTS

Do you know...

* *Teenagers should file tax returns every year and report every dollar earned to create valuable RRSP contribution room...*

* *Tuition and education tax credits can help both the student and the parents...*

* *Every 19-year-old should file their own return to claim the GST Credit...*

* *Child care and moving expenses can often be claimed by a student...*

* *A $500 tax exemption is available on bursary or scholarship income...*

As we speed into the 21ˢᵗ Century, opportunities abound for those with post-secondary education, while those who have not achieved their high school diploma are finding that job opportunities are diminishing and that income is lower than that of educated and skilled workers. It is clear that to avoid low standards of living in the future, or unemployment, education is the key to success.

Such preparation for prosperity in the future, does not come without a cost. According to statistics cited in the February 24, 1998 federal budget, the average debt load of students graduating from a four-year program will be more than $25,000 in 1998. . .not a positive start on the road to prosperity.

As a result, several measures have been introduced under the government's "Canadian Opportunities Strategy," the highlights of which are itemized below:

- Introduction of the Canada Millennium Scholarship Foundation, a $2.5 billion endowment fund available in the year 2000, to provide financial assistance of about $3,000 annually to low- and middle-income students for access to post-secondary education.

- The Canada Study Grants intend to help needy students with dependants, with disabilities or those with very limited financial resources, beginning in 1998-99. Up to $3,000 per year will be distributed to 25,000 needy students with dependants.

- Canada Foundation for Innovation: granting support will be extended, starting in 1998, for advanced research and graduate students at universities, colleges, research hospitals and not-for-profit research institutions, in the area of health, environment, science and engineering.

- Tax relief for student loan interest: a new tax credit for interest on student loans will apply to loans approved under federal or provincial student loan programs, beginning in 1998.

- Tax-free RRSP withdrawals will be allowed for lifelong learning starting in 1999.

- Tax relief will be provided for part-time students through a new education tax credit and child care expense provisions, starting in tax year 1998.

- The Canada Education Savings Grant under the new RESP provisions will provide a grant to provide 20 cents for the first $2,000 invested in an RESP for a child under 18.

- An EI premium "holiday" will be provided for businesses that employ youth between the ages of 18 and 24 during the years 1999 and 2000.

The new tax provisions announced through this initiative, as well as some tax planning tips for filing a return for a student, will be discussed in detail in this part of the book.

68 CONSIDER TAX PLANNING OPTIONS FOR STUDENTS

The single-most significant wealth-creating opportunity young adults have over any other taxpayer is time: time to invest in themselves through their education; time to invest their money to maximize compounding earnings growth and finally, time to weather the economic cycles of the new global, knowledge-based economy.

It is not unusual to think that every 18-year-old has the potential to be a millionaire, based on his or her own productivity and that of the capital that will be invested and saved. In fact, the "Lifetime Millionaire" is really an average Canadian.

A taxpayer who makes $25,000 a year on average over a productive lifetime of 40 years, will have made one million dollars. Under today's tax rates, roughly one-third of that will be taxed away — close to $300,000.

Every parent can set his or her child on the road to financial freedom by teaching basic financial planning concepts, including how to control the taxes children will pay. If each taxpayer could arrange their affairs to reduce their lifetime tax bill by just 10% — $30,000 in the example above — a lifestyle improvement would result.

There are several simple steps to begin a child's journey to lifetime tax savings:

- Plan to accumulate a university fund with both Child Tax Benefit and RESP savings.
- Plan to create future wealth by transferring capital assets to children at an early age.
- Teach your child to win the tax game...starting with the first play.

Take Bailey, for example. A 20-year-old engineering student, she is in receipt of income from a variety of sources: "scholarships" from a Registered Educational Savings Plan (RESP), scholarships from her university, a research grant, and even some income from part-time employment.

Bailey should file her own separate tax return to claim her GSTC Credit, any provincial refundable tax credits she may be entitled to, the determination of available RRSP room so that a contribution may be made to offset scholarship, investment, and employment income, and finally, the computation of tuition and educational credits, which might be transferable to her parent's return.*

The idea, therefore, is to get Bailey's income below the "Tax-Free Zone" — the Basic Personal Amount ($6,456) plus any available Personal Amount Supplement (up to $250 in 1998 and $500 in 1999), all her available tax provisions (deductions for the first $500 of scholarship income, RRSP, investment carrying charges, non-refundable tax credits for CPP premiums, Employment Insurance, tuition, education credits, student loan interest credits, medical expenses, charitable donations, and so on).

---

*Students may also choose to carry unused credits forward to offset their own future income.

Such prudent planning will help to create a transfer up to $5,000 of unused tuition and educational credits for her supporting individuals. These strategies will save the family unit hundreds, if not thousands, of dollars over a student's post-secondary years.

69 REPORT TIPS AND GRATUITIES

Students often work a summer or part-time stint as a waiter, waitress, bellhop, taxicab driver or other position in the personal services industry. Besides their wages, these employees must self-report any tips they make during the course of their employment.

Not only will these income sources create RRSP contribution room (see below), they are also eligible for CPP contributions that the taxpayer can make on a "self-remittance" basis through the tax return. Only teenagers 18 and over can contribute to the CPP.

This is an excellent way to bolster your future retirement or disability pension plan draw.

By the way, for those under 18-year-olds who had CPP premiums deducted at source in error, an overpayment calculation can be completed via the tax return to recover these amounts to you.

70 FILE A RETURN FOR NEW CASH NOW AND IN THE FUTURE

In order to contribute to an RRSP you must have had "earned income" sometime in the past. Many students find they are prohibited from contributing to an RRSP in the first year they are taxable, because the required "RRSP Room" does not exist on Revenue Canada's records. You can rectify this problem by filing returns for past years in which you had part-time earnings, even if you were not taxable.

Every dollar earned, whether by a paper route, pizza delivery, babysitting, or any other part-time job you have had throughout your adolescence, should be reported on a tax return every year to create "RRSP contribution room." You can find this figure on last year's Notice of Assessment from Revenue Canada. This process can help you create tax savings for yourself and your supporting individuals.

Sometime in the future, when earnings may be large enough to be taxable, the RRSP room can be used to create an RRSP deduction. Such a move will not only save tax dollars in the year of contribution, but may create a tuition/education credit transfer of up to $5,000 for a student's parents or spouse, or even an additional child care expense claim under new credits for full- or part-time students.

Remember, the tax-sheltered compounding of the money within the RRSP will grow into a significant retirement fund over time. And for the information of those without disposable dollars, RRSP room can now be carried forward indefinitely.

Finally, remember that even if you are not taxable, filing a tax return might help you collect on refundable federal tax credits like the GST Credit or the Refundable Medical Expense Supplement. So save all those receipts for glasses, contact lenses, dental work, etc.

71 CONTRIBUTING EARLY TO AN RRSP PAYS OFF

There are two reasons most people contribute to an RRSP — the first is to receive an offsetting tax deduction that will reduce taxes payable. The second is to accumulate tax-free earnings within the RRSP.

Investments inside an RRSP make so much sense for a young Canadian. The person who contributes money to an RRSP each year for 40 years, starting at age 20, will likely have the opportunity to accumulate more wealth, even though they invest less money, than their middle-aged counterparts.

In a simplistic example, at an interest rate of 6%, the 20-year-old who contributes $1,000 each year — less than $85 a month — will accumulate $154,761.97 on principal investments of $40,000. The 40-year-old who contributes $333 a month or $4,000 each year for 20 years (or twice the principal–$80,000) will have only $147,142.36.

The net gain, before acknowledging the tax savings made over the years, is almost $48,000 in favour of the 20-year-old: about $7600 more in overall accumulations, *but this is accomplished with only half the principal investment*. It is important to act on this tax tip. The elements of time, rate of return, and tax-free compounding within the RRSP, used to your best advantage, will accelerate your financial freedom, particularly if you start investing early in your lifetime.

72 SHOULD YOU INVEST INSIDE OR OUTSIDE A REGISTERED ACCOUNT?

When it comes to your taxes, there's no such thing as a stupid question. You need to know how tax rules affect your daily decision making. For example, many Canadians don't understand the difference between investing inside and outside of an RRSP, and are too shy to ask!

If you place your investments inside a "registered account" it means that you will likely claim a tax deduction for the full amount of the principal invested (depending on the size of your RRSP contribution room and your income level). In this instance, you are making your investment on a "pre-tax basis." You will receive a tax deduction for your principal and the earnings that your investments make within the plan are sheltered until you withdraw the funds. Then both principal and earnings are included in income. Simple, right?

When you invest in a non-registered account, on the other hand, you are investing with tax-paid dollars. Subsequent earnings are taxed as earned, and withdrawals of principal are not reported on the return.

For these reasons, there is an ordering of choices within your investment vehicles that makes logical tax sense. Those who have taxable incomes and RRSP room, for example, should contribute to an RRSP first — provided they are not restricted by age. (You cannot contribute to an RRSP in the year you turn 70 unless you contribute to the RRSP of a younger spouse.) If you do this you'll receive an immediate return on your investment through tax savings on your return.

Once you have made the decision to invest regularly in an RRSP, it is important to choose the individual investments inside the plan carefully. Your tax sheltered interest earnings, for example, will multiply faster when compared with results from an unsheltered interest-bearing investment outside the RRSP. This is because compound interest earnings outside an RRSP must be reported on the tax return on an annual basis — even though you don't actually receive the money until the principal is withdrawn and interest is paid out to you. A tax bite is taken from all such earnings, in advance, if your income otherwise exceeds the Basic Personal Amount, deductions and other credits.

On the other hand, Canadian dividend or capital gains-bearing assets might be held outside the RRSP umbrella, to take advantage of lower tax rates on these earnings types. You might wish to discuss these basic strategies with your parents or financial planner.

73 CONSIDER OVER-CONTRIBUTING TO YOUR RRSP WHILE YOU ARE YOUNG

To maximize the tax-free growth of earnings inside an RRSP, you may wish to consider contributing more than your "RRSP Room." This is allowed, but with some restrictions. That is, you should plan to keep the over-contribution balance under $2,000, to avoid penalties. You must also be over 18 years old to make an over-contribution.

Such an over-contribution makes sense for young people, who can benefit from lengthier periods of tax-free compounding time. However, there is another catch: in the future you will need to have the required RRSP contribution room to "use up" these extra RRSP contributions. As you now know, without that room, which is based on "earned income" from the immediately preceding tax years, no RRSP deduction is allowed.

Generally this is a smaller problem for students than for those in their 50s and 60s, as students will expect to have employment/self-employment earnings well into the future.

74 MAXIMIZE THE USE OF THE TAX-FREE ZONE

Every person has a right to earn $6,456 — or $538 each month — before he or she is subject to tax.

Starting in 1998 certain taxpayers at low-income levels will qualify for an additional Personal Amount Supplement of up to $250 in 1998 and $500 in 1999 and future years.

Many families waste this opportunity of cashing in on tax-free productivity. By 1999, four people earning $6,956 each can make $27,824 completely tax-free every year, for example. Teach your family members to strive to earn at least this income ceiling every year to maximize wealth within the family unit.

One way entrepreneurs can do this is to hire that student in the family business. Let's say the student, aged 19, earns $5,000. You can deduct this expense from business income, provided work was actually done by the student for a wage at fair market value. All of that income earned by the student is income tax-free. In addition, resulting RRSP room is $900, which can be used next year to make an RRSP contribution. Tax-free earnings will start accumulating in the RRSP immediately, if the contribution is actually made. Further, the RRSP of $900 will reduce taxes payable in the future. Even more tax savings may result with a transfer of tuition/education credits to one of the parents' returns.

As you see, the $5,000 the student earns reaps tax savings in many different ways. Therefore, this circle of wealth creation begins with the personal productivity of each family member.

75 MINIMIZE TAX ON EDUCATIONAL PRIZES

Students who are scholars qualify for a special tax break.

Scholarships, fellowships and bursaries — including net project grants received by artists — qualify for a special tax exemption: the first $500 of such income is tax exempt. Scholarships are usually reported on a T4A slip and then entered on the tax return to Line 130, "Other Income."

Be sure to recover past overpayments if you forgot to claim the $500 exemption. You can do this by requesting an adjustment to your previously filed tax return.

76 TAX BREAKS ARE AVAILABLE FOR EMPLOYED STUDENTS

In 1998 Revenue Canada clarified its policy with regard to employer-paid education. This has led to a retroactive tax break for some employees, as explained below:

Starting in tax year 1997 and subsequent years, certain employer-funded training will no longer be considered a taxable benefit. This includes:

(a) Courses taken for maintaining and/or upgrading employer-related skills, such as fees, meals, travel and accommodation costs paid for courses leading to a degree, diploma or certificate in a field related to the employer's business.

(b) Business-related courses, such as first-aid, stress management, time management, etc., will be non-taxable, as will any in-house training.

Those employer-paid courses that will continue to be taxable to the employee include any courses taken for self-interest that are not related to the employer's business.

For the 1997 year, the T4 slip will have already been submitted to Revenue Canada. It will therefore be necessary to amend these slips to reduce employment income in Box 14 and the benefits reported in Box 40. The employee will have to ask the employer to do this, and then the employee will request an adjustment to the tax return in order to receive a refund of the overpaid tax in 1997. While there will be no impact on EI premiums, there could be an adjustment for overpayment of CPP, which will also be refunded, when Revenue Canada reassesses the tax return.

The employer who refunds the overpayment to the employee can request a refund of the employer's portion of the CPP premiums by completing Form PD24, or asking for the credit to be transferred to the following tax year.

77 STUDENTS QUALIFY FOR A TUITION FEE CREDIT

Students who attend an educational institution providing courses at a post-secondary school level, or an institution certified by Human Resource Development Canada to provide occupational skills, may be eligible for the tuition fee tax credit, which is a non-refundable tax credit. This means the credit is only valuable if you are required to pay taxes.

Starting with the 1997 and future tax-filing years, students who are not taxable may carry forward their unused tuition tax credits to future years, when the credits can be used to offset future taxes payable.

An educational institution generally includes public universities, public or private colleges, vocational schools, and may include a professional organization that provides educational courses to members, as long as one minimum qualification for membership is secondary school graduation. Tuition fees paid must exceed $100 to be eligible for the write-off.

Certain post-secondary institutes *outside* Canada may also qualify for the tuition fee credit provided that courses taken lead to a degree not lower than the bachelor or equivalent level. The course taken must be of not less than 13 consecutive weeks in duration.

The student must be at least 16 years old, and there is no upper limit to the size of the tuition fee credit, but the amount must exceed $100.

Tuition paid for part-time courses, such as night school, will also qualify, as do fees paid for correspondence courses, but in that case only if taken inside Canada.

78 MOST TUITION EXPENSES OF STUDENTS ARE TAX DEDUCTIBLE

Students should be very careful to save receipts pertaining to their studies for use on their income tax returns, as outlined above.

Eligible tuition fees include admission fees, charges for use of a library, charges for use of labs, examination fees, application fees, confirmation fees, charges for certificates, academic fees, membership or seminar fees specifically related to an academic program and its administration, directly supervised flying time and lecture time for those studying to be commercial pilots.

Starting in the 1997 tax year, certain ancillary fees and charges, other than student association fees, will be allowed for the purposes of the tuition fee credit, provided that such fees are required from all full-time or part-time students. This can include athletic and health services fees.

Specifically disallowed are fees levied in relation to property acquired by students, fees for the provision of financial assistance to students or fees for the construction or renovation of any building, unless that building or facility is owned by the institution and used to provide courses at a post-secondary level.

Also ineligible are fees paid for medical care, board and lodging, transportation, parking, tangible goods (slide rules, microscopes, uniforms, gowns), solo flying time, entrance fees to professional organizations or the cost of books, except those used in correspondence courses.

79 TUITION FEES ARE DEDUCTIBLE FOR SESSIONS IN THE CALENDAR YEAR ONLY

Even though you may pay for the tuition fees for your entire academic year in September, only those fees pertaining to studies in the calendar year (January to December) will be claimed on your current year's return.

Therefore, from both a tax and a cash flow point of view, it may make sense to pay tuition fees in instalments.

 # 80 CLAIM THE MONTHLY FULL-TIME EDUCATION TAX CREDIT

Starting in 1998 students may claim $200 a month for each month or any part thereof that they were in *full-time* attendance at a designated educational institute, as a non-refundable tax credit on their 1998 income tax return. (This is an increase from the $150 a month allowed on last year's tax return.) An exception to the full-time rule is made in the case of disabled persons, who by nature of their disability are able to take only a part-time load.

A qualifying educational program for these purposes is one that runs for at least three consecutive weeks and requires instruction or work in the program of at least 10 hours a week. The work involved in the minimum 10 hours a week includes all forms of direct instruction such as lectures, practical training or laboratory work, as well as research time for the purpose of writing a thesis. Usually four full courses or more qualify, although three may qualify if the educational institute ensures the workload satisfies the 10-hour-per-week minimum. Work on essays, term papers and other written work and oral presentations will count.

Further, a registered student spending a majority of time researching for post-graduate studies will be regarded as being in full-time attendance, as will a post-graduate student holding a full-time job if the required research time is spent.

Also remember, most teachers taking summer school will be allowed to claim the education tax credit for full-time or part-time studies (see below).

81 THE NEW PART-TIME EDUCATION TAX CREDIT

Starting in the 1998 tax year, a new education tax credit will be available for those attending school part-time. Part-time students will now be able to claim a non-refundable credit of $60 for each month of part-time attendance at a qualifying educational institute.

Part-time attendance will be defined as a program of study lasting 3 consecutive weeks, and involving a minimum of 12 hours of coursework a month. Eligible students will have to claim either one part-time or one full-time credit for each month, but not both.

This credit will also be used as the basis for a supplementary child care expense deduction, discussed below.

82 TRANSFER UNUSED TUITION FEES AND EDUCATION CREDITS

Students may transfer the unused portions of their tuition fee/education credits to a supporting spouse, parent or grandparent. However, they must first use the amount to reduce their own income to non-taxable status.

The maximum combined transferable amount is $5,000. No amount may be claimed by a spouse who, because of marriage breakdown, is living separately and apart from the student at the end of the year and for 90 days commencing in the new year.

Unmarried students, or married students whose spouse is not claiming the student for the Spousal Amount or any tuition/education tax credits, may transfer the unused amounts to the student's parent or grandparent. The student must designate in writing that the transfer is being made to that person (use Form T2202).

The "parent" can include in-laws, step-parents, natural parents, adoptive parents or someone the individual was wholly dependent upon for support and in whose custody the child was before reaching age 19. Not included are foster parents who received support payments for the child.

It is important to plan to take maximum advantage of the new tax rules for 1997 and future years. For example, now that students can carry forward unused tuition and education credits for use on their own future tax returns, a new question must be asked: is it better to take the tax benefits from the transfer of tuition and education credits to a parent's or spouse's return now, or forfeit those savings in favour of future tax reductions in the student's own hands, later? Also, never transfer more tuition/education credits than your supporting person needs to reduce income, so that the carried-forward opportunity can be maximized.

Given that we are still in a period of extraordinarily high tax rates today, supporting individuals and their students should discuss the benefits of these tax savings now, and invest the tax savings if possible.

83 PART-TIME STUDENTS QUALIFY FOR NEW CHILD CARE EXPENSE DEDUCTION

Child care expenses incurred to enable a parent to go to school will be allowed to offset earned income from employment, self-employment, training allowances, the taxable portion of scholarships, bursaries and fellowships as well as disability pension from the Canada Pension Plan.

Previously such a deduction was limited to those parents who attended school on a full-time basis. Starting in 1998, however, a limited new tax deduction will be extended to part-time students as well.

The deductible amount will be the lesser of these amounts:

1. the actual expenses paid, up to a maximum of $7,000 or $4,000
2. two-thirds of earned income
3. for each month the student is taking education on a part-time basis, $175 per child under age 7 and $100 per child age 7-16.

Part-time education qualifying for this credit will include enrollment at an educational institute in a program that lasts at least three consecutive weeks and involves a minimum of 12 hours of coursework each month.

There is more good news. In the past the child care expense deduction was only available to those who attended post-secondary school. Now even those parents who attend high school courses on a part-time basis, will qualify for the child care expense claim.

84 CHILD CARE EXPENSE CLAIMS INCREASE

The February 24, 1998 budget has also increased the maximum claims for child care expenses for all working parents. The new rules are as follows:

For most taxpayers, the claim for child care expenses, made on Line 214 of the tax return, is a maximum of either $4,000 or $7,000 per child, depending on a number of factors including the age of the child, whether the child is severely disabled, the earned income sources of the parent, and the actual amounts spent on child care.

Usually it is the lower-income earner in the family who is required to claim child care expenses, but when a parent attends post-secondary school, it is possible for the higher-income earner to make the claim, based on that person's actively earned income. For full-time students there is a maximum *weekly* amount of $175 or $100, depending on the age of the child, and/or infirmity. For part-time students, a *monthly* amount of either $175 or $100 is available, as described in Tip 83.

The maximum age of children for whom child care expense may be deducted is "under 16 at any time during the year." The higher deduction limits are for those children under the age of 7 or severely disabled (that is when a Disability Tax Credit is claimable for the child). The lower limits are for those between the ages of 7 and 16, or mentally or physically infirm (but no Disability Tax Credit is claimed).

The resulting claim for child care will decrease net income, and thereby could increase other refundable tax credits (such as the GST Credit, CTB, or provincial tax credits) claimed elsewhere on the return of the student or the supporting individuals.

Under these new rules it is possible that a new child care claim may be created for single parents, a working couple, or a couple both of whom are students, provided that they were both enrolled in a designated educational program at the same time (for at least one week) or for single parents.

85 CLAIM TAX CREDIT FOR STUDENT LOAN INTEREST

According to the February 24, 1998 federal budget, the debt loan for a typical student graduating after four years at post-secondary school has increased to $25,000 in 1998. More than 40% of all graduates have student debt that exceeds $15,000. We also know that approximately 80% of students repay their student loans in full; however, starting out with such large debts can be difficult, particularly if the student is not successful in finding a job right away.

Those facts were the primary reasons behind some new tax relief for students. Starting in 1998, those with student loans under the Canada Student Loans Act or a provincial statute that gives financial assistance to students who study at a post-secondary level, will be allowed to claim a non-refundable tax credit for interest paid on these student loans during the year.

This credit will be available for interest paid in any of the five preceding tax years ending after 1997. For tax year 1998 you will be able to deduct loan interest on existing loans for that year. The carry-forward eligibility will begin with the 1998 and future years.

Let's say, for example, that the student is not taxable in 1998. The student loan interest credit can be carried forward to next year. If next year the student again pays no tax, the student loan interest from 1998 and 1999 can be carried forward to the year 2000. If the 1998 student loan interest is not deducted by the year 2003, it can no longer be used.

86 FILE FOR GST/HST CREDITS TO HELP WITH NON-DEDUCTIBLE DEBT

If you are age 19 or older, married, or a parent, you may claim a GST/HST Credit in your own right, simply by filing an income tax return. You must also be a resident of Canada as at December 31 of the tax year, to qualify. You must not have been in prison for six months or more during the tax year.

If you missed making the claim in a prior year, file now and Revenue Canada will refund the missed credit to you. You can then take those tax refunds and pay off your non-deductible student loans, credit cards or invest in an RRSP or other investment.

87 STUDY MOVING EXPENSE RULES FOR STUDENTS

Students may also qualify for special tax treatment under the provision for moving expenses, a tax deduction that will again reduce the net income on Line 236. If you move to start a summer job, for example, your moving expenses may be tax deductible against those employment earnings, providing you move to take a job which is at least 40 kilometres away from your old residence.

The same rules hold true if you move after graduation to take a job in a new city, or if you move to a university or other post-secondary school — inside or outside of Canada — to study under a scholarship or fellowship, research grant or other similar award.

Foreign students who are residents of Canada may deduct moving expenses from taxable award income received in Canada.

Deductible moving expenses include the cost of selling the former residence, such as real estate commissions, penalties for paying off a mortgage before maturity and legal fees and advertising costs, expenses associated with the new home purchase such as transfer taxes and legal fees, temporary living accommodations for up to 15 days including hotel and the full cost of meals, all removal and transportation expenses for moving the household and all family members and the costs of cancelling an unexpired lease.

Starting in 1998, deductible moving expenses will include the costs of maintaining a former residence, limited to the least of these amounts:

- the actual expenses
- $5,000.

Also deductible are the costs of utility hook-ups and disconnections, changes in drivers' licences or other legal documents requiring an address change.

Non-deductible moving expenses include expenses incurred in house-hunting trips and expenses to clean a rented residence.

Be sure to keep all receipts, because moving expenses are often audited, and are very lucrative in reducing income in the year of the move, or future years, if there is an excess of expenses over income earned in the new location.

CHAPTER 5

NEGOTIATE TAX-EFFICIENT EMPLOYMENT CONTRACTS

Do you know...

* *T4 Slips have changed dramatically in 1998...*
* *Certain benefits paid to relocating employees are now taxable...*
* *Your company car is taxed as a benefit, but certain car allowances are tax-free...*
* *Employees are allowed to claim a deduction for some out-of-pocket expenses ...*
* *The GST/HST rebate on tax deductible expense is missed by most taxpayers...*

It's true that most employees think filing their tax return is relatively simple, especially if their tax filing profile has remained the same over the last several years. In 1998, however, Revenue Canada and the Department of Finance have thrown a few new twists to the returns of the almost 13 million Canadians who report employment income.

For example, certain tax-free benefits extended to employees who were required to relocate, will now be taxable.

Amounts earned by volunteer firefighters or other emergency volunteers will now qualify for a higher tax deduction.

Young people may find themselves in higher demand for work, as a result of the Employment Insurance Premium holiday for employers, starting in January 1999.

As well, the T4 slip itself has been completely changed to enable scanning and imaging technology at Revenue Canada.

Finally, those who use their auto for business use will be able to make a claim for capital cost allowance or leasing costs with a higher ceiling limit.

In the last chapter we also discussed new tax-free benefits for those who have taken educational courses that will benefit their employer's business.

Many don't realize that an employee has lots of opportunity, from a tax-planning perspective, to maximize the investment made in the employer–employee relationship. Here are some suggestions:

- Strive to find ways to minimize the source deductions your employer must make for income taxes.
- Try to utilize all tax provisions that bring tax-free benefits your way.
- Know and claim all legitimate deductions available for any out-of-pocket employment expenses.
- Maximize the opportunities to use up all RRSP contribution room every year.
- Invest any of your tax savings.
- Negotiate future employment contracts with your tax advantages in mind: aim to receive taxable and tax-free perks to enhance your family's lifestyle, and the opportunity to participate in profit sharing plans, which will allow you to earn tax-deferred and tax-preferred capital gains.

88 FIND WAYS TO REDUCE INCOME TAX SOURCE DEDUCTIONS

Your employer is required by law to reduce your gross pay by certain statutory source deductions such as premiums payable to the Canada Pension Plan and Employment Insurance. In the case of income tax deductions, there is some flexibility in the amounts taken from your pay. The first step an employer will usually take is to have you complete a TD1 form. This form will tell the employer what non-refundable tax credits you will qualify for, and from this the tax withholding rate can be determined.

However, it is also possible to have tax withholding reduced during the year. Any time in which the taxpayer will have a significant number of other tax deductions on his or her personal tax return, he or she can apply to Revenue Canada to have source deductions reduced. This can happen if the following provisions will apply in the tax year:

1. Loss carryovers are available
2. The following deductions will be claimed:
   a. Registered Pension Plan deductions

    b. RRSP contributions

    c. Union Dues or professional fees

    d. Child Care Expenses

    e. Attendant Care Expenses

    f. Moving Expenses

    g. Allowable Business Investment Losses

    h. Employment Expenses

    i. Carrying Charges

    j. Repayments of EI, or other social benefits erroneously paid to you

    k. Alimony or Maintenance payments deductible

    l. Northern Residents Deductions

    m. Overseas Employment Tax Credits

3. Any other provisions that will reduce the taxpayer's taxable income.

To reduce your tax withholdings and therefore increase your monthly income, a letter is forwarded to Revenue Canada, requesting that tax deductions be waived on the salary or wages, the name and address of the employer is outlined, and, in the case of alimony or RRSP contributions, the name of the recipient or plan holder is outlined. The employer will then receive a letter of authority from Revenue Canada waiving the requirement for tax deductions on the income in question. The process of obtaining the waiver takes about three weeks.

89 REPORT INCOME FROM MISSING INFORMATION SLIPS

A new T4 Slip exists for 1998. You will find income and source deductions on the left-hand side of the new form, and references to taxable benefits along the bottom. If you have lost an information slip, such as a T4 slip, dig out the cheque stubs or other proof of payment of salary or wages. This income, even if only casual in nature, must still be reported by the taxpayer. It is also important to do so, to create RRSP contribution room which may be used to the taxpayer's advantage in future years. The onus is on the taxpayer to report all income from employment, whether or not a T4 Slip is received.

90 YOU CAN NEGOTIATE FOR CASH OR BENEFITS

If you are negotiating your own employment contract, as most employees do, be sure you know all the tax rules — and be aware that cash is not your only possible remuneration.

The most successful negotiator is not necessarily one who wins it all, but rather one who aims for a win-win settlement. That's why a knowledge of tax-free and taxable benefits can be so lucrative in an employment negotiation. Your employer may be unable to give you a raise but could be quite agreeable to a number of "perks" that will raise your standard of living.

✸ 91   TAX-FREE BENEFITS ARE NICE

Tax-free perks are, of course, the best kind! Consider negotiating for:
- employer-paid education if courses benefit the employer's business
- discounts on merchandise
- uniforms or special on-the-job clothing
- employee counselling for health, retirement or re-employment
- employer-paid costs for an attendant if employee is severely impaired by injury
- subsidized meals
- transportation to and from work
- membership at an athletic or social club
- relocation expenses.

When a raise is out of the question, or the cash a company can offer you is already at its maximum level, it may be easier for your employer to grant you one of these wishes.

92   TAX-FREE AUTO ALLOWANCES CAN PAY OFF

If, under the contract of your employment, you are required to use your car, there are certain instances when an auto allowance, paid to you by your employer, can be received on a completely tax-free basis. For example, if the auto allowance:

(1) is based solely on the number of miles or kilometres you drive to meet your obligations under your contract of employment;

(2) the amount is reasonable; and

(3) no other reimbursement is received to cover auto costs. (However, the employer may pay your costs of supplementary business insurance, parking, toll, and ferry charges without affecting the tax-free status of your auto allowance.)

Therefore, the wise employee will submit a detailed auto log to the employer very year in order to validate the tax-free status of his or her auto allowance.

93 BIRTHDAY GIFTS CAN BE TAX-FREE

One interesting perk of employment can be the receipt of a gift in the amount of up to $100 from your employer. Such a gift can be received tax-free once a year, except in the year of marriage, when a $200 tax-free gift can be received. Unfortunately, the employer will not be entitled to a write-off for the amount either.

Still, leaving hints about your upcoming birthday every year could pay off, if your employer is tax wise...

🟤 94 TAXABLE BENEFITS ARE NOT BAD, EITHER

A taxable benefit is a tangible good or service received from your employer as a form of remuneration. It is reported on a T4, and included as total earnings in Box 14. The employer is required to take off the tax for these perks at the time the value is transferred to you, so you might be a little poorer on the cash side, but living a better lifestyle as a result. Timing is an issue, as is the present value of the perk received.

Negotiating and receiving a taxable benefit can be better, for example, than waiting to earn the after-tax dollars and buying the goods or services yourself. Your employer may be able to offer you the following perks:

- rent-free or low-rent housing
- employer-paid vehicle
- interest-free or low-interest loans
- income tax preparation services
- travel benefits for the family
- tuition fees
- financial counselling
- employer-paid education for the employee's self-interest
- certain relocation benefits
- gifts of consumer goods
- group health or life insurance coverage.

95 MOVING AT REQUEST OF EMPLOYER CAN PAY OFF

If your employer moves you to another part of the country, ask for an Employee Home Relocation Loan. This is an interest-free or low-interest loan designed to cushion the costs of housing at the new city. A taxable benefit will be calculated and included in your income, based on the difference between the current prescribed rate of interest set by Revenue Canada, and the interest rate you are paying for the loan.

An offsetting deduction is allowed on a portion of this taxable benefit for the value of the loan, up to $25,000, computed for a five-year period. This is a tax break that can be lucrative for the taxpayer. However, the most difficult part about this deduction may be finding an employer who'll agree to the plan!

Remember that unreimbursed moving expenses may qualify for a tax deduction. This could include the costs of removal and storage, travelling and transportation costs, costs associated with the new home purchase, such as transfer tax and legal fees, and costs of selling your old home, such as real estate commissions or penalties incurred when paying off a mortgage before maturity. You may even be able to deduct some of the costs of carrying your old residence if you haven't been able to sell it. (See Tip 64.)

For these reasons, it may be a wise move to work out the tax-saving details with a qualified tax professional before packing your bags.

96 CERTAIN RELOCATION BENEFITS NOW TAXABLE

Starting with the 1998 tax year employees who are contemplating a transfer with their employer should be aware of new tax rules that will make some relocation benefits taxable for the first time. This should be taken into account when assessing the costs of the move to the family.

For example, an employee will now be taxed on one-half the amounts received, over $15,000, in respect of the decrease in value of the old residence. Interest benefits derived from the receipt of loans other than the Employee Home Relocation Loan described above, may also be added to the employee's income if it is reasonable to conclude the loan would not have been made, had it not been for the fact that the person was an employee of the company.

Therefore, discuss the tax implications of the remuneration your employer is extending with a tax professional, before accepting the compensation package.

97 SHOULD YOU TAKE THE CASH, OR THE CAR?

Here's a common tax question: Is it better to take the cash, pay the tax and buy your own car, or should you negotiate for an employer-owned vehicle? What are the tax consequences when an employer pays for your auto operating costs? To answer these questions, it is important to understand the tax consequences which, unfortunately, are rather complicated.

When your employer provides a vehicle to you, a taxable benefit is computed for any time the vehicle is used by you or your family for "personal use." Recently, it was also clarified that the taxable benefit will arise whether or not you actually use the vehicle that is made available to you. (However, certain tax reductions could apply.)

The benefit has two components: the value of the vehicle itself, and operating costs relating to the vehicle. While paying the tax on these benefits can sting come tax time, an employer-provided vehicle may be a faster way for you to drive a new car than waiting to accumulate enough after-tax dollars to buy one outright, or take on the risk of financing the purchase or lease yourself.

The benefit is called the "standby charge," and is calculated as 2% per month (or 24% annually) of the original cost of the car where the employer owns the vehicle. If the car is leased, the benefit is calculated as two-thirds of the leasing costs, without including the insurance costs.

If the employer also pays your operating expenses, a second taxable benefit is calculated based on the actual costs of operation relating to personal driving. For 1997 and 1998, the operating benefits will be calculated at 14 cents per kilometre of personal driving (or 11 cents if the principal business of the employee is selling autos), less any amounts the employee reimbursed the employer for operating expenses. (The reimbursement must occur within 45 days of the year end.)

Or, where the auto is used at least 50% of the time for employment purposes, the employee may elect to have 50% of the standby charge added to income, as an operating benefit, less any reimbursements of expenses paid back to the employer. Therefore, 3% per month (or 36% annually) of the original cost of the vehicle is calculated for both the employer-paid operating expenses and the value of the car, times the number of months the vehicle is available for personal use.

Finally, if the car is used at least 90% of the time for employment purposes, the standby charge could be reduced or eliminated if personal use is less than 1,000 kilometres per month. This provision could wipe out your taxable benefit entirely. Check this out with your tax professional, and see Tip 99.

98 CHOOSE THE EMPLOYER-PROVIDED VEHICLE

If you are provided with an employer-owned vehicle whose capital cost is $21,000, your taxable benefit each year will be $5,040 (24% of

$21,000). If you are paying tax at a marginal rate of 42%, this benefit will cost you about $2,100.

If you are also provided with the operating costs, and qualify to choose the 50% of standby-charge election, your taxable benefit would be $7,560 with resulting taxes payable of $3,175.20.

The standby charge, by the way, is always computed on the original cost of the vehicle. Because it does not decrease as the vehicle depreciates, the standby charge can be expensive if you're driving an old car. In these cases, then, it is wiser to be driving a new car, to justify the tax costs. This should be part of your negotiation with your employer.

99 STANDBY CHARGES CAN BE REDUCED

If you use your employer-provided vehicle 90% or more for employment use, and your personal use is less than 1,000 kilometres each month, you can have your standby charge reduced, which will save you money. A special tax calculation will have to be made to justify personal use and submitted to your employer.

Simply take the usual standby charge and multiply it by the number of personal kilometres over 1,000 times the number of days in the month the car was available to you.

For example, let's say the normal standby charge is $5,040, and your personal use driving is only 500 kilometres a month. Your revised standby charge is $5,040 × 6,000 km (personal kilometers driven in the year) divided by 12,000 (1,000 kilometres per month). The result is a taxable standby charge of $2,520, assuming the car was available to you all year long.

The key to this lucrative tax saver is to keep track carefully of all personal/business driving.

100 OR ASK FOR HELP BUYING YOUR OWN CAR

One of the disadvantages of an employer-provided vehicle is what happens when you lose your job or the employer loses the business: no family car.

If this is a concern, you may wish to secure ownership of the family vehicle by asking either for a raise to cover your car payments, or an employer-provided low-interest loan with which to purchase the vehicle, or both.

The benefit of a low- or no-interest loan will be added to your income, and will be subject to tax at your normal marginal tax rate.

However, if you are required by your contract of employment to use your vehicle in your employment and pay all costs, an offsetting tax deduction is allowed for the employment portion of the interest benefit.

To buy a $25,000 car outright, you'll have to earn about $39,500 before tax, assuming a marginal tax rate of about 42% (25,000 × 1.58). If the vehicle's costs are tax deductible, by virtue of your employment contract, it may be wiser to finance the cost of the car, take a deduction for the interest costs — up to a maximum claimable amount of $250 a month or $8.33 a day in 1998 — and use the cash you now have to top up your RRSP. Then use your tax savings from the RRSP to pay down the car loan.

101 LEASING PROVIDES GREAT TAX WRITE-OFFS, BUT NO EQUITY

To some, perhaps the best tax benefits of all arise out of leasing a vehicle. For 1998 maximum claims for leasing costs paid are $650 plus PST/GST/HST, an increase of $100 over last year's amount. The deductible amount is based on the proportion of employment/personal use that was made of the vehicle.

Given that the value of a purchased vehicle for capital cost allowance purposes has increased again in 1998 to $26,000 (plus taxes) you should compare your lease costs to the combined interest and CCA deductions you would have received if you had purchased a vehicle instead.

You may find that the write-offs between an employee-owned and a leased vehicle are similar. However, there are two major differences: timing and return on investment. In year one, only one-half the normal depreciation rate (1/2 of 30%) is allowed on the owned vehicle, based on a maximum capital cost of $26,000 plus PST and GST, as mentioned previously. Therefore, the leased vehicle generally provides greater tax benefits in the first year, depending on when you acquire it during the year.

At the end of the term of the lease, however, you have no capital asset on your balance sheet. If this is of concern to you or your banker, consider investing your tax savings from the lease write-off in another income-producing asset that has potential for appreciation.

Some leases can be structured so that you "buy out" the asset for the amount of the last payment or other similarly small amount that makes it attractive for you to acquire ownership at the end of the lease term. Such an agreement may change the leasing agreement into a conditional sales agreement under which the periodic payments are considered "capital" rather than "operational," and are therefore not fully deductible. Watch out for this.

102 CONSIDER ALL VEHICLE ACQUISITION VARIABLES

The question of whether to buy, lease or negotiate an employer-provided vehicle should be viewed from a cash flow and investment viewpoint; there are many variables to be considered:

1. In general, with an employer-provided vehicle, a standby charge and operating benefit will hit your pocketbook at the very least the end of April in taxes due, or in the requirement to make quarterly instalment payments if your employer fails to make source deductions throughout the year. But you won't have to use your after-tax dollars to pay for operating expenses and financing costs incurred during the year.

2. Choose a self-leased vehicle and you'll generally have the bigger tax write-off in the first year, at least. Also consider that the lease costs and operating expenses must be paid throughout the year with your after-tax earnings: 50- to 60-cent dollars. A steady income and job security is required.

3. If you choose to own your vehicle, your cash flow may be improved over the leasing option, as you'll pay only operating costs and financing charges with after-tax dollars throughout the year. A portion of those operating costs may be recoverable on your tax return. You'll get a deduction for interest and capital cost allowance at year end, which compensates you for the depreciation, and you'll end up with an asset on the books to increase your net worth. If you use your tax savings to pay off your car loan, you'll also have the opportunity to save money on financing charges, although you might consider paying off non-deductible debt or topping up your RRSP first.

Under Option One, you have the use of your pre-tax dollar until April 30, when you must have the money on hand to pay the tax liability. Under Option Two, you must have the income to finance the lease costs each month and wait to get back the tax benefits of your cash expenditures until you file your tax return. Under Option Three, you have to earn the after-tax dollars first before you can afford the car or have the means to finance the purchase.

How does one make the decision? Ask your tax professional to crunch the numbers under each scenario so you can be sure.

103 YOU CAN DEDUCT EXPENSES OF EMPLOYMENT

Employees enter into a master–servant relationship, which is firmly regulated by the Income Tax Act. In general, an employee is not allowed to make tax deductions from income unless it is a requirement of the contract of employment to make out-of-pocket expenditures that are unreimbursed.

Employees also cannot write off the cost of depreciable property, with the exception of capital cost allowance on automobiles, aircraft or musical instruments.

However, under certain circumstances, employment expenses are legitimate and tax deductible. If you are earning a salary, part salary, part commission or commission only, make sure you claim all your tax breaks. The first thing you have to do to make a claim is to file Form T2200, "Declaration of Employment Conditions," which must be signed by the employer.

Take Mike, for example, a high school teacher who runs the continuing education department for the local high school, as well as his normal teaching duties in the woodworking and graphic arts department. He receives a salary of $65,000 a year plus a taxable car allowance of $1,500. At tax filing time, however, he finds his expenses have exceeded this allowance. For his car, including depreciation, expenses total $7,400; 50% of this is employment-related driving according to his auto log. There have also been expenses for meals and entertainment, and Mike is aware that 50% of his $950 in expenses can be claimed on his return. Finally, special supplies expenses, like wall-display materials, stationery, and other office supply items amounting to $350 were not reimbursed. So his eligible employment expenses amount to about $4,500, and at his tax bracket about half of this can be received back in tax savings...very worthwhile indeed.

There's more good news. Mike can also apply for a rebate of GST/HST paid on his income-tax deductible expenses. In fact, because Mike only just became aware of these tax provisions he can request an adjustment for missed employment expenses all the way back to 1985, as well as missed GST rebates back to 1991, the year this controversial tax came into effect.

Remember this, however: these claims will only be allowed if Form T2200 "Declaration of Employment Conditions" is signed by the employer and available with the rest of the schedules when filing your tax return. All receipts should be kept for presentation upon audit request.

104 NEW TAX DEDUCTION AVAILABLE FOR EMERGENCY SERVICES PERSONNEL

A deduction of up to a maximum of $1,000 can be claimed to offset the income received by volunteer ambulance technicians, volunteer firefighters or those volunteers who assist in search or rescue missions of other individuals, or other emergencies, starting in 1998.

This deduction will be considered an "employment expenses deduction" on the T1 return. The deductible amount will appear on the T4 and must be supported with Form 2200.

105 ALLOWABLE EXPENSES FOR THOSE WHO EARN A SALARY

If you are an employee who is paid an hourly wage or salary, complete Form T777, *Statement of Employment Expenses,* to claim the following:
- accounting and legal fees incurred to collect salary or wages
- motor vehicle expenses including capital cost allowances
- travelling expenses, including cost of meals if away for at least 12 hours from the municipality where your employer is located
- parking costs
- supplies used directly in your work
- salaries paid to a substitute or assistant
- office rent
- workspace in the home expenses (subject to limitations).

If you are an employed commissioned sales person you can claim the expenses listed plus some additional ones, listed in Tips 106 and 107.

106 OPTIONS ON CLAIMING EXPENSES AGAINST COMMISSION SALES

A commission salesperson who is an employee may deduct employment expenses based on two options:
1. *Travel expenses only:* This would include auto operating costs plus Capital Cost Allowances (CCA) as well as taxi, bus, rail, air, or other transportation costs if usually required to travel outside of your employer's metropolitan place of business and pay costs; also meals and tips, if you are away 12 hours or more. What's important about this option is that expenses may exceed commissions earned and offset other income in the year.

2. *Sales expenses:* Advertising, promotion, entertainment, auto and travel expenses, as well as certain home-office expenses are claimable. But note, under this option, expenses may not exceed commissions earned, with the exception of CCA and interest on the vehicle.

If you negotiate contracts on behalf of your employer and receive remuneration that includes commissions in whole or in part, you may be able to deduct the same expenses noted for employees in Tip 105 above, plus:

- income tax preparation fees
- advertising and promotion costs
- entertainment and meal expenses for your clients (50% of actual expenses), provided receipts and reasons for meetings are well documented
- meals (subject to 50% rule) and lodging if away for at least 12 hours
- licence and bonding costs
- insurance costs, including liability insurance
- medical underwriting fees
- leasing costs for computers, cellular phones, faxes and other electronic equipment
- cost of courses to maintain, upgrade or update your skills.

✸107 MOTOR VEHICLE EXPENSES OF EMPLOYEES

An employee will generally be allowed to claim motor vehicle expenses and/or travelling expenses if all of the following conditions are met:

- s/he is normally required to work away from the employer's place of business
- s/he is required to pay the motor vehicle expenses
- s/he did not receive a "non-taxable allowance" from the employer (see Tip 92)
- Form T2200 "Declaration of Employment Conditions" is filed.

Again, have the employer sign the T2200 which must be done before any claim for employment expenses can be made. Expenses that can be claimed must be supported by a distance log that charts both business and personal travel. The actual expenses claimed will be prorated based on business travel over total distance travelled. They include the following operating costs:

- gas and oil
- maintenance and repairs
- licence and insurance

- parking (usually claimed in full) and car washes (usually prorated to business/personal use);

as well as the following fixed costs:

- *interest on car loan:* maximum $8.33 a day for new loans negotiated in 1997 and 1998; for loans negotiated in the period from September 1, 1989 to December 31, 1996 this amount is $10.00 a day; from June 18, 1987 to August 31, 1989 the amount was $250 a month
- *leasing costs:* claim a maximum of $650 a month plus PST/GST for new leases negotiated in 1998; $550 a month plus PST/GST in 1997; from September 1, 1989 to December 31, 1996 this amount was $650 a month plus taxes; from June 18, 1987 to August 31, 1989 the amount was $600 a month
- *CCA on vehicle:* this is based on a maximum value of $26,000 plus taxes for new acquisitions in 1998; $25,000 plus taxes in 1997; this was previously $24,000 plus taxes from January 1991 to December 31, 1996; from June 18, 1987 to August 31, 1989 this amount was $20,000; until the end of 1990, the amount was $24,000, without taxes.

108 DEDUCT HOME WORKSPACE EXPENSES

Home workspace expenses are claimable only if the workspace is mainly where you do your work, or you use the workspace only to earn employment income and on a regular and continuous basis for meeting clients.

	Claimable	*Not Claimable*
Salaried Employees:	1. rent 2. utilities 3. cleaning materials 4. minor office repairs	1. CCA on home 2. property taxes 3. insurance payments 4. interest on mortgage
Salary and Commission:	1. 1 to 4 above 2. property taxes 3. insurance	1. CCA on home 2. interest on mortgage

Expenses for workspace in the home must be allocated for employment/personal use through square footage measurement. If the space is 250 square feet and total home space is 1,500 square feet, the percentage of expenses allowed is 17%. It's a good idea to prepare a sketch of the home workspace area and how this compares to the rest of the living space in the home, in case of audit.

Home workspace expenses may not be claimed if the amounts will exceed net employment income after all other expenses are claimed. If, for example, the employee earned $12,000, other expenses were $5,000 and allowable home workspace expenses were $3,000, the full amount of allowable home workspace expenses are claimable. However, if net employment income before calculating home workspace expenses in this case was $2,000, the taxpayer must carry forward $1,000 of the workspace expenses to next year.

109 EXPENSIVE LEGAL FEES MAY BE TAX DEDUCTIBLE

It is usually a difficult and unfortunate event that causes an employee to hire a lawyer to defend his or her rights to income sources or against client grievances.

Certain legal fees are tax deductible:

1. Legal expenses incurred after 1985 to collect or establish a right to a retiring allowance or pension benefits, less any awards for costs, and amounts rolled over to an RRSP.
2. Legal expenses incurred to collect salary or wages owed to the employee by the employer.
3. Legal expenses incurred by employees who sell or negotiate contracts for events that are a normal risk of earning income from employment.
4. Legal expenses incurred to enforce payment of taxable maintenance amounts previously established in a Family Court.
5. Legal expenses paid for assistance in filing an objection or appeal of tax, interest or penalties assessed under the Income Tax Act, a decision under the EI Commission or CPP.
6. Legal fees incurred for the purpose of gaining or producing income from business or property, including your investments.

The following legal fees are *not* tax deductible:

1. Legal expenses incurred for costs in obtaining a divorce or separation agreement.
2. Legal expenses for outlays of a capital nature (add to capital cost).
3. Legal expenses incurred for advice in preparing a tax return unless this is in connection with earning income from business or property, or selling property or negotiating contracts.
4. Legal expenses incurred to protect a real estate licence to earn commissions.
5. Legal fees attributable to an automobile accident that occurred while the vehicle was used for personal purposes.

110 SPECIAL DEDUCTIONS FOR LONG-DISTANCE TRUCK DRIVERS

Those who regularly travel away from their home terminals can deduct the costs of meals and lodging to a maximum of three meals each day; one after every four hours from checkout time. Two methods of claiming expenses are available:

(a) *Detailed:* You must keep a record book itemizing expenses and their receipts. Then claim the actual amounts paid as expenses on the tax return.

(b) *Simplified:* You must keep a detailed list of trips. Then claim $11.00 for each meal. (This "per meal" rate is subject to change but was set at $11.00 at time of writing.) There is a maximum of 3 meals in a 24-hour period, that begins at checkout time. If you travel scheduled runs of 10 hours or less, only one meal claim is allowed for lunch.

Make the claim on Revenue Canada's Form TL2 "Claim for Board and Lodging," and don't forget to claim also a GST/HST rebate for these tax-deductible expenses. The claim for meals is subject to a 50% restriction after February 21, 1994.

111 THE CLERIC'S RESIDENCE ALLOWANCE

A member of the clergy who is a regular minister of a religious denomination and in charge of a diocese, parish or congregation, or engaged exclusively in full-time administrative service by appointment of a religious order or religious denomination, can deduct an amount equal to the value of the residence or other living accommodation occupied by him or her in the course of the office or employment, to the extent that such value is included in computing income for the year. The deduction can be computed based on rent paid or the fair rental value of the residence. However, the deduction may not exceed income earned from employment.

112 ALLOWABLE MUSICAL INSTRUMENT COSTS

If you are an employed musician, check out these tax deductible items on your instruments:

• maintenance and repairs
• rental fees

- insurance costs
- CCA on the instrument.

All expenses are limited to the amount of income earned from your employment as a musician. Recover any GST/HST paid by filing Form GST/HST-370. (See Line 457 on the tax return.)

113 ALLOWABLE EXPENSES OF EMPLOYED ARTISTS

Employed actors, artists, dancers, singers, musicians and writers enjoy special tax deductions for the following supplies used up in the performance of their duties:

- supplies used up (ballet shoes, body suits, chisels, paper, computer supplies)
- workspace in the home
- motor vehicle or travelling expenses.

Claim the lesser of actual expenses incurred, $1,000 and 20% of employment income from artistic activities. The claim is further reduced by any allowable musical instrument costs or CCA and interest on vehicle claimed elsewhere on return.

Note: Motor vehicle and travelling expenses as well as musical instrument costs can be claimed separately on Form T777 to escape the $1,000 or "20% of income from employment" restriction.

114 ELIGIBLE EXPENSES FOR GST/HST REBATE PURPOSES

A portion of the GST/HST you paid on your tax-deductible employment expenses are claimable on Line 457 of the tax return as a credit against total taxes payable. You can apply to receive this rebate for the following eligible expenses, by completing form GST/HST 370:

- accounting and legal fees
- office expenses
- travelling expenses
- entertainment expenses
- meals and lodging
- motor vehicle expenses, excluding interest, licence, or insurance
- leasing costs
- parking costs
- miscellaneous supplies (maps, pens, pencils, etc.)
- membership fees in professional organizations

- CCA on motor vehicles, aircraft and musical instruments.*

Expenses ineligible for the GST/HST rebate include:

- items not deducted on the income tax return
- CCA for any assets except those listed above
- supplies acquired from someone who is not a GST/HST registrant
- expenses incurred outside Canada (i.e., gas purchased in the U.S.)
- zero-rated supplies such as basic groceries, exported goods
- exempt supplies such as insurance premiums, mortgage interest, licence, insurance, interest and registration fees for autos, most educational services.

The GST/HST rebate is one of the most missed rebates on the tax return since its introduction in 1991. If you claimed employment expenses on Line 229 and missed this rebate, file an adjustment to your return with form GST/HST-370 to receive a rebate on your tax-deductible expenditures. GST/HST rebates on operating expenses are reported on Line 104 as income in the year received; GST/HST rebates on capital assets will reduce claims for CCA.

115 BE ON THE LOOKOUT FOR SUBCONTRACTING OPPORTUNITIES

When you negotiate your next employment contract, ask yourself whether there are any barriers to providing additional services to others on a subcontracting basis. A radio disc jockey, for example, might be paid a salary to host a particular show, but might negotiate a contract independently to provide a series of special broadcasts or commercials to unrelated third parties. Will his contract of employment prohibit him from earning extra income outside of the employer's place of business?

Artists and writers often have the opportunity to be both employed and self-employed. If you are a typesetter, is there an opportunity for you to provide typesetting services to others after hours on a subcontracting basis?

Always be on the lookout for subcontracting opportunities. It's a great way to make extra money and create a series of legitimate tax deductions available to the self-employed, provided you are not prohibited by your contract of employment from doing so.

---

* Acquired after 1990 and for which GST/HST was paid. Those taxpayers who lived in Nova Scotia, New Brunswick or Newfoundland were also subject to the HST effective April, 1997.

116 CLEARLY ESTABLISH THE NATURE OF YOUR WORK RELATIONSHIPS

Revenue Canada will frown on transactions that are employer–employee in nature but reported as subcontracting for the potential tax benefits.

You must establish that you are truly an independent contractor, and not connected to the employer through a "master–servant" relationship, by meeting several "tests," including the following:

- you have control over where you work and how the work is done, and you own or rent the equipment or tools
- the work is not an integral part of the employer's business
- you bear the risk of loss and have the opportunity and right to the profits of your activities.

You can also prove your activities are independent by showing that you are providing services to a number of different individuals or companies, and that you have made your own investment in capital assets of your subcontracting enterprise.

As a subcontractor, you will file an income and expense statement to report your net profits to Revenue Canada.

CHAPTER
6

HOW TO PRODUCE INCOME FROM YOUR INVESTMENTS

Do you know...

* *You can make double-digit returns with contributions to an RRSP...*
* *You can use RRSP Contribution Room to reduce tax on retiring allowances...*
* *You can reduce your overall tax burden by diversifying your investments held in non-registered accounts...*
* *You can transfer dividends earned in non-registered investments between spouses...*
* *You can offset capital gains of the year with current or prior year capital losses...*
* *You can maximize individual surtax reductions by earning dividends...*

Proper application of tax provisions will have a critical impact on after-tax investment results, particularly with recent turmoil in the global markets. Market winners will want to maximize RRSP contributions, which have been capped at $13,500 per year until 2003, and shelter the rest of their capital from tax, if possible. Yet others, particularly seniors who turn 69 during the year, face major investment decisions as they are required to mature their RRSP deposits.

The name of the game is tax sheltering and deferral in these years of peak tax rates in Canada. To come out a winner, you may need the help of a sharp tax advisor, an experienced investment planner and a lawyer who together can help prepare an intelligent investment and estate plan for you.

117 USE RRSP ROOM AND CONTRIBUTIONS TO YOUR BEST ADVANTAGE

It is possible that you, like many others in Canada, are carrying forward a sizable RRSP contribution room balance from the years 1991 to the present. The question one must ask is "Why?" Why would you pay more tax than you have to? Why would you miss out on the opportunities to make tax sheltered investments?

When times are good, and you are healthy enough to produce earnings that create RRSP room, try to make the maximum contribution. It will save you big money on your taxes — 26% to over 50% depending on your marginal tax bracket and province of residence. You might even consider taking advantage of over-contribution rules as a hedge against future cash flow problems.

There are times when taking an RRSP deduction may not be in your best tax interest. For example, if you are single and earned less than the basic personal amount (and the new Personal Amount Supplement), you won't be taxable. But, perhaps you have unused RRSP contribution room of $5,000. Should you make a contribution?

The answer is probably yes. The reason is to start cashing in on tax deferred investment earnings. Should you claim the RRSP deduction? The answer is no. Claim the actual deduction in another year when you need it to reduce taxable income. Save the"undeducted RRSP contribution balance" for use in future years.

When should you forego the RRSP contribution? Perhaps when you don't need the deduction to reduce taxable income and you have other non-deductible debt, such as personal credit card balances. Speak to your financial planner for more direction, if needed.

To maximize your opportunities under tax-sheltered registered retirement plans, you must first know what income sources qualify for RRSP earned income (described below). Then make a point of contributing to an RRSP and deducting the contribution in a year when you can get the biggest tax bang for your buck. This will generally be when taxable income is at a high marginal tax rate. Remember, RRSP room can now be carried forward indefinitely into the future. Keep track of that plus all undeducted RRSP contributions.

118 UNDERSTAND WHAT RRSP EARNED INCOME IS

If you had the following income sources last year, you will probably have the required RRSP contribution room to allow you to make a tax-deductible RRSP contribution:

1. Salary or wages before deduction of EI (Employment Insurance) premiums, CPP or RPP (Registered Pension Plans through employment), employee contributions to a Retirement Compensation Arrangement, or the cleric's residence deduction;
2. Income from royalties of works by an author or inventor;
3. Net income from carrying on a business where the taxpayer is actively engaged in daily operations alone or as a partner;
4. Net rental income;
5. Net research grants;
6. Supplemental unemployment insurance benefits;
7. Taxable Child Support payments or repayments included in income, (generally based on pre-May 1, 1997 agreements) or support payments received by a spouse;
8. Employee Profit Sharing Plan allocations (Box 35 of the T4PS);
9. After 1990, income received from a CPP/QPP disability benefit.

LESS:

Refunds of salary, wages, or research grants, union dues, professional dues, other employment expenses on Line 229, net losses from carrying on an active business, net rental losses, alimony or child support payments deducted or repaid, and amounts included in business income on account of the disposition of eligible capital property, which represent additional negative balances in excess of recaptured deductions.

The result is "earned income." The lesser of 18% of earned income or the maximum dollar limitation (see below) is your current year's maximum RRSP contribution.

119 KNOW WHAT YOUR MAXIMUM DOLLAR LIMITATION IS

In order to contribute the maximum allowable dollar amount into your RRSP, you must earn the following:

Tax Year	Maximum Dollar Limitation	Earned Income Needed*	In Year
1991	$11,500	$63,889	1990
1992	$12,500	$69,444	1991
1993	$12,500	$69,444	1992
1994	$13,500	$75,000	1993
1995	$14,500	$80,556	1994
1996-2003	**$13,500**	**$75,000**	**1995-2002**
2004	$14,500	$80,556	2003
2005	$15,500	$86,111	2004

*This represents prior year income levels needed to contribute the maximum-dollar ceiling to an RRSP.

After 2005, maximum ceiling levels will be indexed to growth in the average industrial wage in Canada.

🟊 120 KNOW HOW MUCH RRSP CONTRIBUTION ROOM YOU HAVE

Your RRSP contribution room is based on the prior year's earned income, this year's maximum dollar limitation, and whether or not you contribute to a registered pension plan at your place of employment. If you do, your contribution room will be reduced by a "PA" or Pension Adjustment amount. You can find this figure in Box 52 of your T4 Slip, or Box 34 of a T4A of the immediately prior year.

The contributions you make to your company's registered pension plan will always be linked to your RRSP contribution room under current tax rules. The 1998 RRSP contribution will be affected by PAR (Pension Adjustment Reversals). This can happen in cases where employees leave their jobs without all the pension benefits that were previously used to limit RRSP room. Check with your employer to determine RRSP eligibility. Qualifying taxpayers will have until April 30, 1999, to contribute to an RRSP for 1998.

In addition, any unused contribution room from prior years (starting in 1991) will increase your current room. The easiest way to find your RRSP Contribution Room for the current year is to look at last year's Notice of Assessment from Revenue Canada, but as described below, this may not be all the information required.

121 MAXIMIZE PREVIOUSLY UNUSED RRSP CONTRIBUTION ROOM

Gather the following information before making an RRSP contribution:

1. Unused contribution room since 1991 (based on 1990 earned income);
2. 18% of your earned income from the immediate prior tax year;
3. Prescribed maximum contribution dollar levels (as described in Tip 119);
4. Any Pension Adjustment (PA) amount, for those who belong to a Registered Pension Plan or Deferred Profit Sharing Plan (RPP or DPSP), or for 1997 and future years, any PAR;
5. Any amounts that qualify for tax-free transfers over and above the normal limitations;
6. Actual undeducted contributions made in the current or prior year;

7. Designated amounts to be used as a repayment under the Home Buyers' Plan.

Once calculated, allowable RRSP contributions can be "topped up" in the current tax year or within 60 days of the current tax year end.*

Check your Revenue Canada Notice of Assessment for your RRSP contribution room first. But if you failed to file a tax return in the past, have a pending reassessment on your tax return, or have qualifying income for tax-free rollovers, (described below) the amount you can contribute to an RRSP will differ from the figure on the Notice of Assessment.

 122 COMMON SOURCES ELIGIBLE FOR TAX-FREE TRANSFERS TO AN RRSP

Make plans to defer taxes by "rolling over" or contributing the following sources of income to an RRSP:

1. Retiring Allowances, for service after 1988 and before 1996, a single limit of $2,000 per year of employment may be contributed. For employment before 1989, the limit is $2,000 for each year of employment plus $1,500 for each year in which none of the employer contributions to a company pension plan is vested in the taxpayer. (This may happen in periods of temporary or short-term employment.) Note that for service after 1995, the government has abolished the $2,000 per-year-of-service tax deferral completely. This will leave your retiring allowances paid for post-1995 service subject to income inclusion in the year received, in full. Try to negotiate the receipt of the retiring allowance over two tax years, if possible, to minimize tax in those cases, or negotiate the continuation of tax-free or taxable benefits after you retire.

2. Refund of Premiums received on death of a spouse or common-law spouse, or in some cases, a supporting individual.

3. Lump-Sum Payments out of non-registered foreign pension plans for services performed while not a resident of Canada.

4. RRSP commutation payments directly transferred to another RRSP.

5. Excess amounts from a RRIF directly transferred to the RRSP.

 123 SEVERANCE ROLLOVERS WILL NO LONGER ATTRACT MINIMUM TAX

Tax-free rollover of retiring allowances into an RRSP will no longer attract minimum tax for amounts received after 1993. You may find a refund in your mailbox from Revenue Canada if you previously received a severance package in 1994-1997 and paid minimum taxes. The amount

---

*This 60-day period can be extended by the Minister.

will depend on whether you previously used a minimum tax credit to off-set regular income taxes in years after you received the severance package.

124 USE SPOUSAL RRSPS TO YOUR MAXIMUM ADVANTAGE

A great way to reduce the taxes you'll pay in later years, and to maxi-mize refundable tax credits in the future is to plan now to split income from RRSP accumulations between spouses. Each spouse may contrib-ute to an RRSP based on his/her own RRSP contribution room, which was built with actively earned income sources.

In addition, though, it is possible for a high-income earner to make an RRSP contribution for a spouse who may not have earned income — perhaps during child-bearing years. In such cases, a portion of or all of the RRSP contribution may be made to an RRSP in the name of the lower earner, with the added benefit that the higher earner can still take the tax deduction. This is called making a "Spousal RRSP" contribution.

Later, in retirement, or in a year when the spouse otherwise has a lower income, withdrawals from the RRSP will be taxed in that lower-income earner's hands. However there is one catch. That is, that the RRSP accumulations cannot be touched until three years from the last spousal RRSP contribution. Otherwise, earlier withdrawals will be taxed in the hands of the higher-income earner and that would likely defeat the whole idea behind the RRSP Spousal Plan.

Spousal RRSP withdrawals also create capital that is attributed to the lower-income earner, with the result that subsequent investment earnings from these amounts will be taxed in that lower earner's hands. Therefore by depositing money into a spousal RRSP you will open a multitude of income-splitting opportunities — all within the frame-work of the law — in the future.

125 DIVERSIFY YOUR INVESTMENT PORTFOLIO FOR MAXIMUM AFTER-TAX EARNINGS

As explained in Tip 3, investors earning dividends and capital gains outside of an RRSP still enjoy lower marginal tax rates on their invest-ments than those with interest income. Marginal tax rates will vary from province to province, with different income sources and within age groups, so check yours out with your tax advisor.

Individuals with taxable incomes in the $35,000 range may be surprised to know that interest earnings, such as those reaped from investments in Canada Savings Bonds or term certificates, are taxed at a marginal tax rate of approximately 40% (or more in some provinces). That is, about 40 cents out of every dollar earned on that investment goes back to the federal and provincial governments by way of taxes.

The same is true of the taxation of RRSP or RRIF withdrawals. Because both principal and earnings must be added to income in full, it is particularly important to plan around marginal tax brackets for different income "benchmarks."

There is much you can do to keep taxes out of the hands of the government. For example, often you can plan to generate only enough earnings to keep a taxpayer in the family under the Personal Amounts. For example, if one spouse has little or no income, while the other is in a high tax bracket, withdrawals up to the Basic Personal Amount ($6,456 for those under 65), plus the new Personal Amount Supplement will be received on a tax-free basis. Seniors may increase these thresholds with the Age Amount.

Alternatively, if one spouse is in a 50% bracket and the other in a 27% bracket, it will generally make sense to earn interest income or take RRSP or RRIF withdrawals in the lower earner's hands first. The higher earner should continue to shelter earnings within registered plans as long as possible, and attempt to earn investment income in non-registered plans in the form of dividends or capital gains.

Also remember that tax on capital gains held outside an RRSP/RRIF will only be paid on disposition of the asset — increases in the value of the assets will not be taxed before then. This gives you a significant tax deferral opportunity — if you are comfortable with the inherent risks attached to some of these assets.

The structure of our tax rates provides a compelling reason for some taxpayers to diversify their investment portfolio. It pays to speak to tax and investment advisors about your options.

126 MAXIMIZE BOTH INCOME AND CAPITAL YIELDS

When you invest in an income-producing asset held outside an RRSP, you usually have two opportunities to make money: through the earnings of the investment (interest, dividends, rental income, business income) or through the capital appreciation of the asset itself (i.e., when you sell the asset, hopefully for more money than it cost to acquire and keep it).

Most common "debt obligations" — Canada Savings Bonds, Guaranteed Investment Certificates, term deposits — do not provide an opportunity for capital appreciation. Interest is earned in return for the use of your money over a period of time.

To assess the effectiveness of an investment strategy, investors need help from their advisors in developing the proper asset mix that will coincide with their need for income capital growth and risk tolerance. It is important to pay attention also to the tax bite when overall investment returns are anticipated. Interest accruals must be reported annually, meaning that Revenue Canada gets its revenue on the earnings before you do; as well, interest earnings are included in income in full, on top of all other income of the year. So, there is both tax and inflation risk with this type of investment.

T-Bills may afford you the opportunity for both interest earnings and capital appreciation. However, shares or mutual fund investments trading on the stock market or investments in a private Canadian corporation may yield "dividends," as well as capital appreciation — or depreciation. Publicly traded securities, or other privately held properties can accumulate value without attracting tax and this may give you some tax advantages now.

For this reason the proper "asset mix" will take into account most forms of investment risk and tax savings opportunities. Speak to your tax and investment advisors about the right strategies for you.

127 UNDERSTAND THE REPORTING OF INTEREST ON CANADA SAVINGS BONDS

Volatility in the marketplace may cause some investors to hesitate making long-term decisions, but nonetheless, for various reasons, it is usually a good idea to consider parking some of your money in interest-bearing investments. For example, it may be convenient to purchase a Canada Savings Bond through a payroll plan at work. (Don't forget to write off your interest charges in this case.)

The easiest way to consider the reporting of Canada Savings Bonds held outside a registered plan, is to determine three things:

1. Are the bonds producing interest on a Regular or Compounding basis? Regular interest amounts will be automatically reported annually.
2. If Compounding, interest earned will generally be reported annually, except in three very specific Series, described below.
3. What group of bonds do they fall into?
   (a) *Series 27 — 35* (all matured): their interest was reported when received.
   (b) *Series 36 — 41* (all matured): these were to have been reported annually or at least triennially.

(c) *Series 42 — 44:* these compounding bonds have to be reported at a minimum of every three years, but the taxpayer
can choose to start reporting annually at any time and for any
number of bonds. In the year reporting is changed, all previously unreported interest must be "caught up" and reported.
Series 42 matured in 1997 and Series 43 matures in 1998 and
Series 44 must be reported on a triennial basis in 1998.

(d) *Series 45 (1990 issues and onward):* these bonds, compounding or regular, must be reported on an annual accrual basis
and a T5 slip will be issued.

128 T-BILLS CAN BE A VIABLE ALTERNATIVE INVESTMENT

Treasury Bills are issued at a discount. For tax purposes, the difference
between the issue price and the value at maturity is reported as interest.
If you sell before maturity, calculate the interest component as follows:

$$\text{Effective Yield} \quad \times \quad \frac{\text{Days Held}}{\text{Days in the Year}} \quad \times \quad \text{Purchase Price}$$

If you sell the bill before it matures, you may also incur a capital gain
or loss. Compute this as follows: Take the proceeds of disposition less
interest accrued during the period held, and reduce this figure by the
adjusted cost base. The result is the capital gain or loss. For example:

1. Cost of T-Bill at discount is recorded: $15,000
   (Maturity Value is $18,000)

2. Interest earned on the T-Bill to date: $ 2,000

3. Calculation of Capital Component:
   Proceeds of Disposition: $21,000 (a)

Adjusted Cost Base:	Cost	$15,000	
	Interest	$ 2,000	
			$17,000 (b)

4. Capital Gain (a – b) = $ 4,000

129 AVOID THESE COMMON ERRORS IN REPORTING INTEREST INCOME

Taxpayers can and do make errors in reporting interest earnings. Here
are four common ones:

1. Most taxpayers miss reporting interest on tax overpayments to
   Revenue Canada. This is shown on Revenue Canada's Notice of
   Assessment.

2. Compounding Canada Savings Bond interest can be double reported if records on prior-reported earnings are not kept.
3. Interest is always reported by the person who earned the original principal; use this rule in the case of interest from joint accounts.
4. In the year a taxpayer dies, claim interest earned to date of death only on final return. The accrued portion of triennially-reported investments that pertain to years other than the year of death, may be reported as "Rights or Things" on an elective return in the year of death. This will enable the estate to claim another set of personal tax credits, and save the tax on some or all of these earnings. All other amounts of interest earned after date of death are reported by the beneficiaries or by the estate.

130 CLAIM THE DIVIDEND TAX CREDIT AGAINST RETURNS FROM CANADIAN CAPITAL STOCK

Dividends represent the after-tax profits distributed by a corporation to its shareholders. The corporation already has paid tax on these profits, so the individual shareholder receives a dividend tax credit for the taxable dividends reported on the tax return, in order to avoid double-taxation. The actual dividends received are "grossed up" by 25% to attain their "taxable" status. Then the dividend tax credit is calculated as 13.33% of this grossed-up taxable dividend, and used to reduce federal taxes payable.

In 1998 and future tax years, this dividend tax credit's value has increased. That's because the government announced a reduction in the Federal Individual Surtax on Schedule 1 of the Return. This surtax is based on "Basic Federal Tax," which is reduced by the dividend tax credit. High-income earners in particular may wish to diversify income sources to get in on the surtax reduction, which will not be available for those whose taxable income exceeds $65,000.

131 TRANSFER DIVIDENDS EARNED BETWEEN SPOUSES

The dividend tax credit is useful only if there is taxable income. It can't be carried forward, so for that reason it may be of benefit for a spouse with a low income to transfer dividend income and the related dividend tax credit to the higher-income earner. This is allowable, but only if certain conditions are met.

If your spouse has little or no income, consider having this person invest monies received in their own right in dividend-producing stocks.

Provided you can create or increase a Spousal Amount elsewhere on the tax return, you can transfer both the dividends and the dividend tax credit to the higher-income earner's return. Prepare your family's returns both ways to determine the best benefit.

132 CREATE A CAPITAL GAIN RATHER THAN ORDINARY INCOME

In general, a capital gain will occur when you dispose of an income-producing asset for more than it cost to acquire it (including the cost of improvements). A capital gain is reported on Schedule 3 in full. It is then reduced by current-year capital losses, if any. In general, 75% of any remaining gains are added to income on page 1 of the T1 General. For some specific types of assets, the $500,000 Capital Gains Deduction may still be available to offset such a gain. This deduction would be taken on Line 254. In addition, transfers of certain publicly traded securities after February 18, 1997 to a favourite charity could qualify for a 37.5% income inclusion.

A capital gain may also occur when there is a "deemed disposition." For example, when a person dies, it is considered that all assets are disposed of at their fair market value immediately before death. If the asset passes to you, that fair market value at the time of death is your acquisition cost.

To compute capital gains or losses, take the proceeds of disposition (which can be sales proceeds or Fair Market Value on deemed dispositions) and subtract from this the Adjusted Cost Base of the asset (which can be its original cost plus all improvements, a specific Valuation Day value, or for many of those who previously made capital gains elections, the elected value). Finally subtract from this any outlays or expenses of the sale, such as real estate commission. The result is your capital gain or loss.

Remember that accrued values on capital assets are never taxed until disposition. This provides a method of sheltering wealth accumulations.

133 AVERAGE THE COSTS OF IDENTICAL PROPERTIES AND STOCK SPLITS

Taxpayers sometimes purchase shares of the same or identical class of the capital stock of a corporation, but at varying times. As well, they may sell such identical shares at varying times and at varying prices. Such transactions within the same group of shares requires the computing of an "average cost" of the shares each time there is a purchase, in order to properly compute any future gain or loss on disposition. A similar procedure is followed for units.

To calculate average cost, determine cost of the shares in the group and divide by the total number of shares held. For shares held before 1972, special rules for valuation apply.

Note: On a stock split, the average cost is affected, but no capital gain or loss transaction occurs until the taxpayer actually disposes of some or all of the shares.

134 OFFSET CAPITAL GAINS WITH CAPITAL LOSSES

It would be great to hold only winners, but the reality is, most portfolios also hold a few losers. You can minimize your capital losses by realizing them in a year you sell other winners — perhaps your rental property or other stocks — if this otherwise makes sense.

Capital gains of the year can then be offset by any capital losses incurred. If you have no other capital gains in the year, allowable losses must be either carried back for use against capital gains in the previous three tax years, or carried forward indefinitely. It is generally best to carry such losses forward if you previously offset gains with the capital gains deduction.

In the year of death on the final return, it is possible to offset other income of the year with unused capital loss balances. Offset capital gains of the year first. Then, before any excess losses can be applied against *other income* of the final year, they must be reduced by previously claimed capital gains deductions. For this reason, it may be wiser to carry back excesses for use against unsheltered *capital gains,* if any, in the previous year.

135 CAPITAL GAINS ELECTIONS CAN STILL SAVE TAX DOLLARS

The February 22, 1994 federal budget eliminated the $100,000 Capital Gains Deduction for most capital assets. As a result, capital gains on disposition of assets acquired after February 22, 1994 will be added into income without the benefit of this lucrative deduction. You may recall, however, a special provision called the Capital Gains Election, which allowed you to elect to report accrued gains from the time of acquisition to February 22, 1994 at an amount between the adjusted cost base and the Fair Market Value at February 22, 1994. The election was made on the 1994 tax return.

In the 1995 tax year, accrued gains on the eligible capital property of businesses whose fiscal years, ending in 1995, included the February 22, 1994 date, also qualified for an election.

The offsetting Capital Gains Deduction was then applied to this deemed gain, creating a virtual tax-free accounting of the assets' increased values. For most assets, these "deemed" proceeds of disposition are used as the new "Adjusted Cost Base" for future capital dispositions; for others, such as mutual funds, an "exempt gains" pool was created, to be used to reduce future gains on those assets. (For more information on post-election calculations, see Tip 158.)

It is now too late to make a late-filed election. Previously filed elections could only be amended or revoked until December 31, 1997. So that leaves us with the residual effects of this provision — an ability to reduce current year capital gains on previously elected assets, by using the provisions of the February 22, 1994 election. Make sure your tax professional and your executor are aware of the existence of the election. Otherwise, you or your estate could be paying taxes of thousands of dollars too much in some cases.

136 AUDIT-PROOF YOUR CAPITAL ASSET VALUATIONS

You might be required to obtain a Fair Market Valuation (FMV) of capital assets you own to determine your "Proceeds of Disposition" in the following instances:

- to justify the figures used on your capital gains election
- upon transfer of capital property to another individual
- upon death of the taxpayer, which triggers a "deemed disposition" of assets
- upon immigration to or emigration from Canada
- upon change of use of assets from personal to business use or vice versa
- to calculate a principal residence exemption when a second residence is disposed of.

The onus of proof for the valuation rests with the taxpayer. To justify FMV when you report such a capital disposition to Revenue Canada, document the following information meticulously:

- for publicly traded shares — stock market quotations on date of disposition
- securities of private corporations — business valuations by certified expert

- real estate — newspaper listings, appraisals, land registry, property tax assessments, municipal records
- art, stamp, coin collections, newspapers — dealers, appraisers, catalogues.

If your asset acquisition dates back to pre-1972 days, obtain valuation as of December 31, 1971 (December 22, 1971, in the case of publicly traded shares).

137 SAVE TAXES WITH LABOUR-SPONSORED VENTURE CAPITAL TAX CREDITS

A federal tax credit is allowed for investments in approved shares of the capital stock of a prescribed labour-sponsored venture capital corporation at any time during the year or the first 60 days of the new year.* For shares acquired in 1998, the federal credit is 15% of the cost of the shares up to a maximum of $5,000, for a maximum of $750. An equal credit is available in some provinces.

These investments are also RRSP-eligible, so the taxpayer may in fact also take an RRSP deduction for the same investment. This "triple header" tax credit makes some investors think favourably about placing some dollars into these funds. However, the terms for investment are often lengthy (in fact, there is an eight-year holding period and in some provinces, a "cooling-off" period which prohibits the claiming of a similar tax credit for the year of redemption or either of the next two tax years). These restrictions should be taken into account, particularly if the investments are held inside an RRSP.

138 TURN NON-DEDUCTIBLE INTEREST COSTS INTO DEDUCTIBLE ONES

In certain cases, Revenue Canada allows taxpayers to write off their investment expenses as they are incurred. This can include interest on money borrowed to make investments in assets held outside a registered account.

Before incurring any new debt it can pay to look at turning current non-deductible debt into deductible debt. It is possible, for example, that your largest non-deductible interest payment is your mortgage.

You can create deductible interest by starting a home-based business and writing off a portion of the interest pertaining to the home office, as previously described. Or you can actually pay off your mortgage and then remortgage and use the money for investment purposes.

---

*This 60-day period can be extended by the Minister.

Any such transaction should only be attempted after seeking professional help to compute the net benefits, based on your projected investment return, mortgage interest rate, remortgaging fees, projected asset mix held outside your RRSP/RRIF, the marginal rate of the tax savings on the interest expense, and Revenue Canada's specific rules for tax deductibility (see below).

Your deductible interest can be used to offset other income of the year, without limitation. This will increase your tax refund, which can be reinvested in new investments or used to pay down your debt.

★ New in '98 139 REVENUE CANADA'S LIMITATIONS ON INTEREST EXPENSE DEDUCTIONS

The general premise of interest deductibility is that there must be a potential for the earning of "ordinary income" from business or property—business profits, interest earnings, dividends, rents—in order for the amounts to be deductible.

You'll notice what's missing in that list—the earning of capital gains or capital gains dividends. Interest on a loan acquired for the purposes of earning capital gains only will generally not be allowable as a deductible carrying charge.

This is important news for those parents who wish to borrow money to buy mutual funds that generate capital gains for their minor children. Interest deductibility will not be allowed if the only income source is capital gains dividends.

Interest on a loan taken to buy shares in a corporation will generally be allowed, if there is potential for the earning of dividends. However, the courts have taken a harder line in some cases, and disallowed the interest deduction despite the presence of the potential for dividend income. The outcomes in each case have depended on factors like taxpayer intention at the time of the investment, share structure, and other specific factors.

Revenue Canada has not required the proration of interest deductions in cases where a mutual fund, held outside an RRSP, produces interest, dividends, foreign income or other "ordinary income sources" in addition to capital gains dividends. Therefore, there is no prohibition of the tax deductibility of interest expenses incurred from a loan to buy equities, provided there is potential for "ordinary income" sources to be generated within the fund.

140 INTEREST ON DIMINISHED ASSET VALUES

In general, there must be potential for earnings from a business or property in order for interest to be deductible. The taxpayer must also be able to trace the borrowed funds to an underlying asset that will earn income such as interest, dividends, rents, or royalties. What happens when the value of that asset diminishes or is lost through insolvency? Will interest on existing investment loans still be deductible?

Fortunately there are some special rules here. Revenue Canada will look at the current use of borrowed funds in assessing interest deductibility. Usually, it is considered that one has stopped using the principal for the purpose of earning income when the property is sold or otherwise disposed of. But if the taxpayer has used borrowed funds to acquire shares in a corporation that has subsequently become bankrupt, or whose value has diminished substantially, a continued interest deduction may also be available.

Tax rules introduced on August 30, 1993 give a tax break when the source of income to which the interest relates no longer exists, effective on losses of source of income after 1993. The portion that has been lost is "deemed" by Revenue Canada to continue to be used for the purpose of earning income from property. This interpretation renders future interest payments on that loan deductible.

To calculate the deduction that applies to such a property, determine the total amount of borrowed money outstanding just before it stopped being used to earn income less the amount of borrowed money that is not considered to be lost.

The amount considered "not to have been lost" is the borrowed money traceable to the amounts received on disposition, if the property was disposed of at fair market value. Otherwise, the amount considered "not to have been lost" is the amount that would have been received if the taxpayer had disposed of the property at fair market value.

On that basis, interest expense deductions will continue to be allowed.

141 CLAIM YOUR SAFETY DEPOSIT BOX AND OTHER CARRYING CHARGES

The following "carrying charges" are deductible against other income of the year, yet are frequently missed by both taxpayers and their advisors. Look back to see if you have receipts to justify the following:

- safety deposit box fees
- accounting/record-keeping fees pertaining to investments
- Canada Savings Bonds payroll deduction fee
- insurance policy loan interest
- interest expenses for loans taken for investment purposes
- for assets held *outside* an RRSP or RRIF:
  - investment counsel fees
  - management fees
  - safe custody fees.

142 HEED THE NEW RULES FOR RRSP/RRIF/RESP FEES

RRSP or RRIF administration fees are no longer tax deductible as carrying charges. This could cause you some bookkeeping headaches come tax time.

RRSP/RRIF "management fees" are usually paid for custody of your securities, maintenance of your accounting records or fees based on the value of your assets. If these amounts are paid from within the RRSP, there is no tax consequence. If you usually give your carrier a cheque for the $125 or $150 it normally costs for these services (also called trustee fees) there will be no tax write-off as in the past.

However, a tricky little provision exists in these cases. Payment of fees with money coming from outside your RRSP will be considered a tax deductible RRSP *contribution*...which is only meaningful if you have RRSP contribution room. This also means that the payment of such fees — which can be fairly extensive in the case of wrap accounts — will be subject to the $2000 over-contribution limit. So get some professional help with this.

And here's a red flag! Payment for management fees of a RRIF must be considered a non-deductible personal expense, as any contributions into a RRIF will deregister it! So pay these fees with the assets within the plan.

Finally, the government has also moved to clarify that, effective the 1998 tax year, RESP fees paid will also be non-deductible.

143 USE ALL OF YOUR ASSETS TO CREATE INVESTMENT POSSIBILITIES

Talent and opportunity, used hand in hand, can help you create wealth quickly. For example, if you are a talented employee, consider asking your employer for a low- or no-interest loan. You'll be taxed on the difference between the rate of interest your employer charges you (which could be nil) and the current prescribed rate of interest (which is based on 90-day Treasury Bill yields). At recent low interest rates this could be the benefit of the century! A repayment schedule will be required.

However, the loan can be used to help you inch closer to your financial goals. If invested in income-producing assets, the taxable benefit you are assessed on the loan (check your T4 Slip) is tax deductible as a carrying charge on the tax return.

Alternatively, you may possess a life insurance policy that has built up a cash value. If you borrow against this cash value, any interest paid back to the policy becomes tax deductible if the loan is used for an income-producing property.

144 ACCOUNT FOR YOUR CNIL BALANCE TO AVOID SURPRISES

The year 1988 was the one in which CNIL was introduced — Cumulative Net Investment Losses. CNIL arises when the investment expenses you have deducted since 1988 exceed investment income reported in the same period. When this happens, the CNIL balance will be used to reduce any available Capital Gains Deduction in the year a qualifying capital disposition is reported.

Since the removal of the $100,000 Capital Gains Deduction in 1994, the only taxpayers who still have to be concerned with CNIL are those who will sell Qualified Farm Property or Small Business Corporation Shares in the future.

For example, assume a taxpayer borrowed $20,000 in 1988 to purchase shares in a Small Business Corporation. From 1988 to 1997, he claimed interest expenses of $8,000, and no other investment income.

(a) He can deduct the interest expenses when they were incurred.
(b) He has a CNIL of $8,000.

Upon sale of his shares in January of the current year he realized $40,000 on disposition of the shares. His $20,000 capital gain qualifies for the $500,000 Capital Gains Exemption. The actual deduction must first, however, be calculated by taking into account the CNIL balance of $8,000.

7

CREATE WEALTH WITH YOUR PERSONAL PROPERTIES

Do you know...

* *Profits from the sale of your principal residence are tax exempt...*
* *Renting out a portion of your home can help you create wealth...*
* *Rental income qualifies as earned income for RRSP purposes...*
* *You can minimize taxes paid on revenue properties...*
* *There are tax advantages if you transfer assets to children...*

Someone once said that the biggest mistake you can make is to believe you work for someone else. Only you can build your own financial legacy through the priorities and commitments you select and decisions you make.

To lead your family to financial freedom, consider these three steps:

1. Prepare a definite financial goal or vision, both for the short and long term;
2. Develop a well-thought-out action plan to help achieve your goals;

3. Recruit outstanding professional resources to help you maximize your options.

A common choice in the road to financial freedom is the acquisition of one or more residences. June and Tom, for example, have secured a fine home, with a substantial mortgage to chip away at. While this seems to consume a large portion of their monthly resources, Tom and June wanted to make their money work for them, instead of the other way around. Was the purchase of the home the right decision? How can they make their current efforts pay off in the long run?

145 REVIEW THE FAMILY TAX CONSEQUENCES OF ACQUIRING REAL ESTATE

Buying a family dwelling can be a good tax-planning decision, particularly if other factors — such as good price, good location, and an upward-moving market environment — all work in tandem.

Whether you own a single dwelling, duplex, condo, cottage, mobile home or other property, disposition at a value higher than original cost plus improvements will generally be taxable as a capital gain — except in the case of your principal residence. Gains accrued in your primary residence can be earned on a tax-free basis, to a maximum of one tax-free residence for a family unit. (See Tip 146.)

The acquisition of second and third residences, however, may require a certain amount of planning to avoid a large tax liability upon your demise, or when you transfer or sell the property to someone else, including your family members. Remember, Revenue Canada considers a "deemed disposition" at Fair Market Value occurs in the following circumstances: (1) immediately prior to date of death, (2) at a time when assets are transferred to persons other than your spouse, (3) when there is a change of use of an asset from business to personal use. Resulting capital gains, if any, may sometimes be deferred with special elections.

Also, watch market trends to make sure transfers at FMV are made at the most advantageous time from a tax point of view. When you know and understand these rules, you can quickly turn your family investments into wealth producers.

146 INVEST IN A TAX-EXEMPT PRINCIPAL RESIDENCE

Many seniors today are wealthier than their parents, for several reasons including enhanced pensions through the Canada Pension Plan, Old

Age Security, company pensions and RRSPs, as well as the fact that many own, rather than rent, their own homes.

Every family unit may hold one tax-exempt principal residence at any given time in a year. That is, any gains on the disposal of a principal residence can be received tax-free, provided that you have not claimed a Capital Cost Allowance (CCA) deduction on the property while you owned it, and you do not have more than one principal residence at a time.

Prior to 1982, each spouse in a family unit could own one tax-exempt principal residence. Often the husband owned the cottage and the wife the house, or vice versa. On subsequent sale of each property, the resulting gains were tax exempt.

It is therefore possible that in such cases, where two residences have been held and maintained since before 1982, each may have a "tax exempt" component. In such cases be sure to seek experienced assistance in preparing Form T2091 Designation of Principal Residence.

147 SAVE A DOWN PAYMENT FOR YOUR STARTER HOME OR COTTAGE

While saving for a new home may seem overwhelming, it's really not so difficult. To begin, get a sense of how much of a down payment you need. Then, determine how much you can save and earn to help you get there in the least possible time frame. It's possible that by filing a tax return in the most advantageous way, Revenue Canada can help you with your homebuying.

If you'd like to save $25,000 for a down payment, for example, you'll need to earn an extra $50,000 (if you're in a 50% tax bracket) to make your investment appear. You might crack this nut — with tax savings from an RRSP.

If you have RRSP contribution room, invest the tax savings you reap from your RRSP contribution in an accumulating fund that builds into a downpayment. If you qualify to contribute $12,500 to your RRSP, for example, you'll save $6,250 each year in taxes payable at the same marginal tax rate of 50%. At that rate, it will take you less than four years to save for your home or cottage ($6,250 × 4 = $25,000), if you consider there will also be investment earnings on the $6,250 you save and reinvest each year.

In order to qualify to make a $12,500 RRSP deduction, you have to earn $69,444 in the immediately preceding tax year, or have substantial RRSP Room carried forward since 1991. This could be a challenge if you make $40,000 at your job. You could take on a part-time job, rent out a portion of your current home, diversify passive investments or start a small business in order to bolster your earnings. Productivity is the key.

You and your spouse could also take a joint approach: make a list of all consumer spending that can be eliminated. Instead, invest these savings in the home or cottage fund. If you both work at a job or self-employment venture, use your spouse's after-tax earnings in their entirety to save for the project, if you can otherwise afford to do so.

Or, if you already have RRSP accumulations, tap into the benefits of the RRSP Home Buyers' Plan. . . .

★ 148 TAP INTO THE TAX-FREE RRSP HOME BUYERS' PLAN

When it was first introduced, the RRSP Home Buyers' Plan enabled a buyer to withdraw up to $20,000 in the RRSP on a tax-free basis to acquire a qualifying home in the period February 26, 1992 to March 1, 1993. This provision was extended to allow "excluded withdrawals" to be made in the period December 2, 1992 to March 1, 1994. Under these old rules no tax-deductible RRSP contribution could be made in the year in which a home buyer's withdrawal was made.

New rules introduced with the February 22, 1994 budget extended the plan again — this time for *first-time home buyers only*. These are people who have not owned a principal residence in the five calendar years before making a withdrawal from their RRSP.

Further changes were announced in the February 24, 1998 federal budget. Starting in 1999, individuals may participate in the HBP *more than once in a lifetime* if certain conditions are met, including:

• previously withdrawn amounts have been paid back
• this happened before the beginning of the tax year.

Contributions made within the 90 days of a home buyer's withdrawal will not be deductible unless a balance equal to or greater than the withdrawal remains in the RRSP.

Any amounts withdrawn under this plan must be repaid on a non-deductible basis over 15 years (1/15 each year), starting in the second calendar year after the year of withdrawal. Also, a contribution made within 60 days of the end of that year can be applied to the previous year. If you participate in 1999, your first repayment must be made by March 1, 2002. The taxpayer may choose to repay the amounts more quickly than scheduled, if desired. However, if you miss making at least these minimum repayments, an income inclusion for any shortfall will result. You can make your RRSP contribution and then designate what portion should be applied to the HBP repayment on Schedule 7.

You cannot designate a Spousal RRSP contribution as a repayment of the HBP, or any amounts of direct rollovers, such as retiring allowances. It is not necessary, though, to have an RRSP deduction limit in order to designate a repayment.

For those who wish to participate in the plan in 1999, the procedure begins with an RRSP withdrawal using Form T1036. This form is given to your RRSP issuer, who will then know not to withhold any taxes from your withdrawal. To qualify you must be a resident of Canada and you must have entered into an agreement to buy a home or to build one. Finally, you must buy or build your home before October 1, 2000.

If the home buyer emigrates or dies, the balance owed at the time of departure or death will be included in the home buyer's income. In the latter case, the surviving spouse can elect to assume the repayment schedule to avoid this liability. However, the election can only be made if

- only the deceased was participating in the HBP
- only the surviving spouse was participating (but the deceased had applied)
- the spouses each had identical repayment periods.

Where the participant becomes a non-resident, no tax inclusion will occur if the balance outstanding is repaid before filing a tax return for the year of departure and within 60 days of becoming a non-resident. After 1997 no repayments are allowed after the end of the calendar year in which you reach 69 years of age. Also check into any additional, tax credit-producing "home buyers' plan" that may be available in your home province.

★ 149 HOME BUYERS' PLAN CAN NOW BE USED BY DISABLED TAXPAYERS

There is good news for disabled taxpayers or those who look after and support the disabled, as a result of the February 24, 1998 federal budget. Beginning in 1999, withdrawals from an RRSP under the newly enhanced Home Buyers' Plan are not limited to first-time homebuyers if the following circumstances exist:

- The individual who is making the HBP withdrawal qualifies for the Disability Amount and the withdrawal is made to enable the individual to acquire a home which is more accessible, or that is

better suited for the personal care or needs of the individual; or
- An individual related to a disabled person who qualifies for the Disability Amount withdraws an amount under his or her HBP, either to acquire a home for the benefit of their disabled relative *or* to help that disabled relative to purchase a home that is more accessible and/or better suited to the personal needs and care of a disabled person.

These changes will help disabled taxpayers and/or their relatives to tap into the funds of RRSP accumulations to provide for better care at home over the long term.

150 WRITE OFF YOUR HOME OWNERSHIP COSTS

Once you have saved the downpayment for your home or second residence, put that property to work for you. By arranging your affairs, you could have new income sources subsidize at least a part of your mortgage payments, taxes and other operating expenses.

You might run a small business out of your home. In that case, you can deduct a portion of your mortgage interest, property taxes, utilities, repairs and maintenance, insurance and other supply costs, based on the square footage of the home workspace, over the total living area in the home.

Provided you do not claim Capital Cost Allowance on your home as a home workspace deduction, your principal residence exemption will stay fully intact. In the meantime, you will be using these legitimate tax deductions to reduce the tax you pay on the small business venture.

151 RENT OUT A PORTION OF YOUR HOME

If practical, you can have others supplement your home ownership costs. You might, for example, also decide to rent out a part of your principal residence. In general, when you start using your residence as a rental property, you are deemed to have disposed of that portion of the property at a fair market value. Such a disposition can have tax consequences when you subsequently sell the home, or if you have selected another residence to be the "principal residence" in the pre-rental period.

However, there is no deemed "change of use" if the portion of the home that is rented is minor, no major structural changes are made to accommodate tenants and no deduction is taken for Capital Cost Allowance (CCA) on the rented part. In this case, your tax-exempt principal residence status is preserved completely.

Any time your home or part of it is converted into a self-contained domestic apartment used to rent to tenants, that part of the home will no longer qualify for the tax-exempt status, even though no CCA claim is made.

You may also move out of the principal residence and earn rental income from it for up to four years as long as you do not designate any other property to be your principal residence in this period and again no Capital Cost Allowance deduction is made on the property. This election may be extended beyond the four-year period in cases where your employer requires you to relocate to a new temporary residence at least 40 kilometres away, as long as you return to your original home before the end of the year in which your employment ends (see later comments).

152 MAXIMIZE YOUR RENTAL PROPERTY EARNINGS TO CREATE NEW MONEY

For those taxpayers who have invested in a rental property that is not also a principal residence, take note of the following tax savings rules, which can help you minimize the taxes payable:

1. Rental income and expenses are usually reported on a calendar-year basis, using the cash method.
2. Net income is first calculated by reducing gross rental income by operating expenses.
3. Operating expenses that exceed gross earnings create a rental loss, which can be used to offset other income of the year.
4. Capital Cost Allowance may be claimed to reduce net income to nil; however, CCA may not be used to create or increase a rental loss.
5. CCA is claimed at the taxpayer's option. Therefore, depreciating a building far below its market value may result in a recapture of previously taken CCA deductions upon disposition of all the assets in the class.
6. Claiming CCA on a principal residence disqualifies the property (or the portion of the property upon which CCA is claimed) from its normal tax-exempt status.

Net rental income is eligible "earned income" used in calculating RRSP contribution room.

153 BE SURE TO AUDIT-PROOF YOUR RENTAL INCOME

Revenue Canada has become particularly concerned with those who write off rental losses against other income, from enterprises that include rentals to relatives or other non-arm's length persons. To avoid unpleasant reassessments in the future, be sure that you are using Fair Market Value pricing in all rental charges. Know what the income level for similar rental properties is in the same neighbourhood. Document this with newspaper clippings of ads for vacant rental spaces, or listings by real estate or leasing agents. Keep all receipts and documents.

154 VACANT LAND CAN BE INCOME-PRODUCING

Taxpayers who earn rental income from vacant land can claim property taxes and interest only to the extent of rental income reported — again, no rental loss can be created or increased with these expenses. They may, however, be added to the land's adjusted cost base for use in calculating any subsequent capital gain or loss on disposition.

However, if the vacant land is held without any rental income being collected, interest and property taxes can neither be deducted nor added to the adjusted cost base.

155 KNOW HOW TO TRANSFER ASSETS AMONGST FAMILY MEMBERS

Taxpayers often wish to pass their residences on to other family members. You can do so during your lifetime (*inter vivos*) or it may be forced upon the family by virtue of your death, when a deemed disposition at Fair Market Value (FMV) is considered to have taken place.

At death, tax-free transfer can be made between spouses. That is, on the final return assets can be transferred to the spouse at their Adjusted Cost Base (ACB) if you wish. In the case of taxable properties, your executor may elect to transfer the asset to your spouse at its FMV, if this is to the family's advantage.

In general, all transfers to children must be at the asset's Fair Market Value. On the final return the difference between the ACB and the FMV is reported by the owner as a capital gain, except in the case of a principal residence, when the resulting gain is considered to be tax exempt.

When you transfer taxable assets to your spouse or children during your lifetime you must be very careful to avoid the Attribution Rules on the subsequent use or sale of the asset by your dependants.

Sales of taxable property transferred to your spouse will result in attribution of the capital gains back to you, unless you have previously elected to transfer the property at FMV and paid the tax at that time. Alternatively, you could set up a bona fide loan which is repayable by your spouse, within 30 days of the year end, and interest is set, charged and paid at least at Revenue Canada's prescribed rates.

Capital gains on sales of property transferred to your children are handled differently.

156 THERE ARE TAX ADVANTAGES OF ASSET TRANSFERS TO CHILDREN

It makes sense to give to your minor child or grandchild a mutual fund or other capital asset instead of a Canada Savings Bond or GIC, particularly if the asset's value is at a current low.

This is because the Attribution Rules do not apply to capital gains income on disposition of assets transferred to a child. While you'll have to report the original transfer of the asset at Fair Market Value for your tax purposes, the child then reports the resulting capital gains on the future sale of that asset. Timing of this transaction can therefore be matched to each person's best tax advantage.

Unfortunately, though, certain income sources, including interest or dividends earned from the gift of a capital asset to a minor child will be taxed in the hands of the adult who gave the gift, until that child turns 18. Therefore in giving assets that have capital, rather than income growth potential over the years to age 18, income splitting can be achieved and the child can benefit from the tax-deferred accrued investment gains, until actual disposition.

157 ENHANCE INSURANCE PROCEEDS TO COVER TAX ON ASSETS

In the year a taxpayer dies, s/he is considered to have disposed of all capital property immediately prior to death, usually at fair market value. Such a valuation will generally invoke a capital gain or loss. In the case of depreciable property (property upon which a Capital Cost Allowance deduction could be taken), it can also create a terminal loss or recapture, depending upon the amount of the Undepreciated Capital Cost (UCC).

The executor often has a series of choices to make in this valuation exercise in order to minimize tax on the final return of the deceased, and to plan the future tax position of the beneficiary of the assets.

Remember, assets can usually be "rolled over" to a spouse at their Adjusted Cost Base — what the deceased acquired it for plus any capital additions while s/he owned it — or UCC, if depreciable. A special election may be made to choose FMV if this is to the family's advantage.

With the removal of the $100,000 Capital Gains Deduction, capital gains on second family residences or other assets could result in expensive tax liabilities. Consider enhancing life insurance coverage for the surviving spouse to protect your assets from being sold by your children in order to pay the resulting capital gains taxes. Professional help should be sought to forecast the approximate amount of tax and insurance coverage necessary in these cases.

Also be sure that all unused capital losses incurred during your lifetime are carried forward, to offset capital gains generated by the "deemed disposition at death" rules.

158 USE THE CAPITAL GAINS ELECTION INFORMATION

In the 1994 tax-filing year, taxpayers and accountants alike struggled with the complexity of the Capital Gains Election. With all the calculations filed and in place, it is now important to know how to interpret them for future use.

Here's how to use the new Adjusted Cost Base information, if you must report the disposition of an asset upon which you made an election:

1. If the property is an interest in a flow-through entity, such as a mutual fund, the elected capital gains will form part of an "exempt gains pool," which will shelter capital gains that flowed out after February 22, 1994. These offsetting amounts will be subtracted from capital gains on a special line on Schedule 3: Capital Gains and Losses, but only until the year 2004.
2. In most other cases, the Adjusted Cost Base of the asset will be the amount of the elected "proceeds" designated in the election, less any non-eligible gain in non-qualifying real property. This refers to the portion of the capital gain in non-commercial real estate that accrued in the period March 1992 to February 1994.
3. For non-qualifying real property that is designated a principal residence after 1994, the original adjusted cost base will be used in calculating the gain on actual disposition. The principal

CHAPTER
8

START YOUR PRE-RETIREMENT PLANNING

Do you know...

* *Taxes have been reduced on retiring allowances...*
* *You can ask for certain perks of employment to continue past retirement...*
* *You can custom-design your pension benefits to minimize taxes...*
* *You can claim special tax provisions if in receipt of foreign pensions...*
* *You can influence the size of your public pension benefits by planning now...*
* *You can negotiate a tax-free death benefit...*

People often ask, when is the best time to begin your pre-retirement planning. The answer? With every new dollar you make, with every career move you contemplate, and with every investment you initiate. The reason? The future is now.

Consider this conversation I had with our children's great-grandmother before she died. On her 90th birthday, I asked her "How does it feel to be 90?" She replied with her trade-mark chuckle: "I don't feel one bit different today than I did when I was 16...it's only my body that seems to be letting me down in some ways."

To me this reply only underscored how quickly time flies. . .blink and one day your baby turns 18; blink again and you're celebrating a 25th wedding anniversary; blink yet again and you are facing the death of a dearly beloved parent. All very natural processes; all instances when baby-boomers contemplate the second and final half of their lives.

Pre-retirement planning forces a contemplation of the meaning of work, family and lifestyle, both now and after our bodies let us down. For some, this phenomenon occurs sooner rather than later. Loss of life or health is devastating; however, it is less so when one is financially prepared. The best time to do pre-retirement planning is when one is healthy (and seemingly invincible!).

That's one of the problems with the whole concept...when times are good, there's no deadline to meet. Nobody has to have a financial plan by April 30 every year! So the motivation to take charge of the future you envision for yourself requires both reflection and commitment on an ongoing basis. How long are you going to work, how much money is enough for the lifestyle you want to have, and what personal price must you pay to make those dreams a reality?

The key is to work smarter and not harder, and one way to do this is by utilizing all tax-planning opportunities to add value to the time you spend making money. Value-added productivity: that's the result of the ongoing process of pre-retirement tax planning.

159 PRESERVE YOUR ASSETS

The length and difficulty of our journey through life can, to a large degree, determine the quality of life we will have in our retirement years. If we are lucky enough to keep our health, our personal productivity can help us achieve a higher level of security or independence. However, if disability, death, divorce or other major misfortunes have come our way, our financial resources must produce the earnings to determine our lifestyle.

The truth is, for many years the most important income-producing asset most people have is themselves! One of the most important steps in creating wealth and maintaining it, to the extent to which you have control over such things, is to preserve your health throughout your lifetime. *Plan* to be productive and healthy. Regardless of age, your family's living standards will suffer if you don't take care of yourself.

160 INSURE YOUR MOST IMPORTANT ASSETS, INCLUDING YOURSELF

Funny, how people think. Most will have no problem agreeing that their vehicles must have annual check-ups, go through maintenance programs and be insured in case of loss or damage. How many of us feel the same way about our well-being?

While you have your health, you must think about what will happen to your living standards when you no longer can produce. Insure yourself for the possibility of disability or death. It is important to have financial resources at hand for the periods in your life when your actively generated income earning capacity has stopped or ended.

From a tax point of view, this is also wise. For example, the life insurance policy proceeds you leave for your family in the case of your untimely death, will be completely tax-free to your beneficiaries. For some, it is difficult to come up with the after-tax dollars to fund such a policy. However, you might consider taking the tax savings from your RRSP investments and turning them over — at least in part — to the investment in a life insurance product. Speak to your financial advisors about your options. Remember, the time to buy life insurance is when you are healthy. It's tough — or incredibly expensive — to get insurance if you are afflicted with a serious illness or old age.

Insurance for disability is just as important. While there is some protection under the Canada Pension Plan, and in some cases, the Employment Insurance Plan, receiving the benefits can take a long period of time, while the government determines your eligibility. By making plans to contribute premiums to a private disability insurance plan, benefits, when needed, can be received on a tax-free basis. Premiums paid, however, are not tax deductible in this case.

If you have an opportunity to contribute to a wage-loss replacement plan through your employment, be sure to enquire about the details of the plan, should you need to draw from it. Will benefits be taxable? Will benefits continue until you are able to do exactly the same job, or will they discontinue if the insurance company deems you are fit to work again — at any job? Some planning for all of these possibilities will certainly pay off, as you don't want to be negotiating when you are at your weakest — or sickest.

161 NEW DEDUCTIBLE GROUP INSURANCE BENEFITS AVAILABLE TO FAMILY BUSINESSES

In the past, unincorporated small business owners could not deduct supplementary insurance coverage for health care items such as prescriptions, dental or eye care as a business deduction. Instead, such amounts paid for the proprietor or his/her family would be claimed as a non-refundable tax credit.

Based on the proposals of the February 24, 1998 federal budget, self-employed taxpayers or members of an unincorporated partnership can take a business deduction for premiums paid to a private health plan on behalf of the individual, his/her employees and his/her spouse, or children, within certain limitations. This new provision will be in effect for fiscal periods ending after 1997

Amounts paid for private health coverage will be deductible if equivalent coverage is extended to all permanent, full-time, arms-length employees. By arm's length, we mean someone who is not related to the taxpayer. This includes employees who have accumulated at least three consecutive months of service with the individual (other than on a temporary or seasonal basis).

To qualify, the proprietor must also be "actively engaged" in the business or be an active member of the partnership. There are also income limitations. The self-employment income must comprise at least 50% of the individual's total income for the year, *or* the individual's income from other sources (not including self-employed or partnership income) may not exceed $10,000 in order for premiums to be deductible as a business expense.

A second restriction applies to the classification of the employees covered by the plan. If the majority of them are related payments will be deductible to a maximum of $1,500 for each of the individual and his/her spouse, and $750 per child. If non-related employees are in the majority, these limitations will not apply and full deductibility of premiums will result.

In some instances, it may be better to claim these premiums as medical expenses on page 3 of the T1 General. This would be true especially for low-income taxpayers, given the introduction of the Refundable Medical Expense Supplement, which came into effect for the first time in the 1997 taxation year. This supplement is available to Canadian residents 18 or older at the end of the tax year, who had at least $2,500 in employment or self-employment income (net of expenses) and allowable medical expenses on Line 332 of the return. A maximum credit of 25% of medical expenses or $500 may be claimed, depending on family net income level.

Small business owners must make provisions to take care of themselves, their family and their businesses should early retirement be forced upon them due to illness or disability. This is one way to prepare for retirement when the unexpected happens.

162 NEGOTIATE YOUR SEVERANCE PACKAGE UP FRONT

Have you ever tried to negotiate overdraft protection when you're unemployed, or a line of credit after posting a business loss? It can be difficult, if not impossible. It can be equally difficult to negotiate a retiring allowance once you've been laid off or terminated. It's when times are good that you should look to the future and negotiate the terms of your "golden handshake."

Revenue Canada has allowed a special tax deferral (explained below) for those who receive a "retiring allowance," which can include severance pay, unused sick leave, termination damages and legal fees deductibility. As this can be one of the biggest financial transactions of one's lifetime, employees will want to make sure Revenue Canada does not take back a big chunk of the retiring package at tax time. Therefore, planning retirement packages well in advance can pay big rewards in tax savings.

163 BACK PAY CAN RESULT IN TAX PAIN WITHOUT PROPER PLANNING

Sometimes, contract negotiations, particularly with a large union, can result in the payment of benefits retroactively. For example, in 1998, the issue of pay equality was being negotiated, for certain government employees to access a potential billion dollar payout. At the time of writing, the outcome had not yet been confirmed.

A payout similar to this could have several components: back pay of employment income, an interest component, and possibly a pensionable component, which could affect the Pension Adjustment calculations. Proper tax management of these one-time amounts is essential, particularly for older workers, who will count on these funds to enhance their retirement nest egg. Here are a few tips:

Lump sum payments received for back pay are generally taxed as income. Such income would create RRSP room, accessible the year following the payment, subject to the normal Pension Adjustment calculations within the Registered Pension Plan provisions, as mentioned above.

It might be tax-wise to ask for the lump sum to be paid out over two tax years, 1999 and 2000, for example. Spreading the lump sum payment over two tax years could keep this taxpayer on the right side of tax bracket increases. In addition, RRSP Room created by the 1999 payment could be used to offset the Year 2000 payment. Or, the interest income component, if any, could be split over two or more tax years, to reduce the tax burden on this portion of the payout.

It always pays to prepare a tax plan well before the money is received, in cases such as this. Other income sources (for example the generation of capital gains receipts or RRSP/RRIF withdrawals) can then be better managed to produce a more tax efficient result over the long term. You may wish to generate only minimal income from such sources, or at very least plan to offset capital gains with losses in the year the payout occurs.

The same sort of planning should occur before an employee receives a severance package from the employer. In this way, debts can be managed well in advance to maximize tax savings provisions, such as the tax-free rollover of severance into an RRSP.

✸ 164 DEFER TAX ON YOUR RETIRING ALLOWANCE WITH AN RRSP TRANSFER

One of the most important aspects of pre-retirement planning is the orderly receipt of retiring allowances. It is often surprising how few people take the time to analyse the tax consequences of receiving $40,000, $50,000, $75,000 or more as a lump-sum final payment. With a little tax planning this very important asset can be sheltered from tax erosion.

For example, a taxpayer is allowed to roll over, into his or her own RRSP, a portion of a retiring allowance received up to a maximum of $2,000 per year of service after 1988, and before 1996. An additional $1,500, for a total of $3,500, may be transferred for each year of service prior to 1989, in which an employer's contributions to a company pension plan had not vested in the taxpayer. This could have happened during a period of temporary employment with your company.

Any remaining balance of the retiring allowance you've received will be "ineligible" for contribution to the RRSP and will be, as such, fully taxable, in the year received.

The February 24, 1998 federal budget made some important changes to the taxation of severance package rollovers into an RRSP. Previously, such rollovers attracted minimum tax at certain income levels. This amounted to an expensive hit upon retirement, as described below.

✱ 165 WATCH OUT FOR THE MINIMUM TAX

The minimum tax is a special calculation, performed "off the tax return" on Form T691. The minimum tax was introduced in the late 1980s to ensure that those who take advantage of otherwise legal "tax preferences," such as the RRSP rollover for severance on termination, would pay at least a minimum amount of tax. Then a recovery process was available. That is, minimum taxes paid in one year could be used to offset regular taxes for up to seven years in the future.

Now here's the good news. Minimum tax will no longer apply in cases where severance packages have been rolled over into an RRSP. This new budget proposal will apply to tax years after 1993. Therefore, those who retire in the future have a much simpler and less expensive tax obligation. Those who retired after 1993 and paid the minimum tax can expect a refund from Revenue Canada, provided they hadn't previously used up the "regular tax offset."

166 OFFSET ANY UNSHELTERED RETIRING ALLOWANCE WITH YOUR RRSP ROOM

In Tip 164 we mentioned that often only a portion of a severance package may be rolled over into an RRSP, depending on years of eligible service. In such cases, "ineligible" portions of the severance must be added to income in full. This can often mean 40-50% tax rates.

There are ways to reduce this huge tax burden. For example, in the year you retire, you will likely have an opportunity to make a "regular" RRSP contribution, based on your accumulated "Unused RRSP Contribution Room." If you've received a retiring allowance that exceeds the tax-deferral limitations discussed above, this untapped "room" can save you money.

Let's say, for example, that you qualify to receive a $25,000 retiring allowance, of which $16,000 is transferable into your RRSP. The remaining $9,000 must be added into your income in the year received. You may be able to negotiate the receipt of the non-eligible allowance in January of the new year, so that it forms part of your income in the next tax year when your overall earnings may be lower.

The eligible $16,000 is first reported as income on the tax return, and then the $16,000 transfer is reported as an RRSP deduction. This rollover will not offset the normal RRSP contribution room.

Now assume you also have RRSP contribution room of $8,000. By investing the ineligible portion of your severance package into the

RRSP, you can create a deduction to offset the ineligible income. In our example, this additional $8,000 tax deduction will offset all but $1,000 of the retiring allowance. These moves will ensure that most of your retiring allowance stays in your pocket now. You will also be in a position to control the level of taxation on your RRSP accumulations in the future, with astute planning of withdrawals. It's easy, it's legal, and all it requires is action on your part several months before you settle your severance package.

167 CONSIDER NEGOTIATING FOR RETIREMENT COUNSELLING SERVICES

You are probably already convinced that it doesn't pay to skimp on the tax advice you need when negotiating your retirement package. Here is more good news: your employer can provide you with the money to seek retirement counselling, including financial counselling, on a tax-free basis. This is a perk that should be negotiated when you receive your employment contract at the start of your relationship, if possible.

You might also ask for — and receive — memberships to recreational facilities on a tax-free basis, or the payment of premiums for private health services, or even a low-interest loan, to continue even after your employment terminates, as described below.

168 KEEP INCOME AND BENEFITS FLOWING AFTER TERMINATION

It is not uncommon for employees to negotiate a consulting contract with their former employer after their employment ends. This could put you into a self-employment status, with a completely new tax filing profile. Net self-employment income also qualifies for the purposes of building RRSP Room, so that you can continue to enhance your retirement savings if you choose entrepreneurship as a future path.

It may also be possible to negotiate for the continued use of certain taxable benefits before you leave your employer or for some subcontracting work. (Usually a T4A Slip would be issued some tax time.)

But you must be very careful. Revenue Canada could disallow the tax-free RRSP rollover of your severance package if they determine that you didn't really "retire." Subsequent consulting contracts must not be a replacement of the employment you previously had.

Therefore you must be able to show your full independence. This could be done by subcontracting with other clients, for example.

169 NEGOTIATE A TAX-SHELTERED DEATH BENEFIT FROM YOUR EMPLOYER

When negotiating an employment contract, prepare for your family's future by enquiring about the possibility of receiving a death benefit. Such a lump-sum payment might be made to your spouse or dependants as a recognition of your service, should you pass away while on the job.

There is a lucrative tax exemption on death benefits paid by the employer: the first $10,000 received by your dependants is not subject to tax.

If your death benefit exceeds $10,000, plan to have the excess paid out over a period of years, which will minimize the tax your dependants will pay on the unexempted or taxable amounts.

While all income sources are appreciated during the stressful events surrounding the death of a loved one, a lump-sum death benefit is particularly advantageous if it can be received to offset the otherwise non-deductible costs of a funeral.

170 MAXIMIZE CPP BENEFITS FOR YOURSELF AND YOUR SURVIVORS

It is important to factor any CPP Benefits into your pre-retirement planning activities, particularly in view of recent enhancements to the future of the plan. By the time you reach age 60, you can choose to tap into your Canada Pension Plan to receive a retirement benefit. Or, if you can, wait to age 65, or even 70, when retirement benefits must start. The amounts receivable depend upon the contributions you make to the CPP during your lifetime, and how early you start receiving benefits. When the benefits begin, they become fully taxable.

When a contributor to the Canada Pension Plan passes away, the spouse will qualify for a Lump-Sum Death Benefit and a Survivor's Benefit. Both of these amounts are taxable to the *survivor* in the year to which the payment relates, or the lump sum may be claimed on a return filed by the estate.

Dependent children will also qualify to receive Orphan or Child Benefits. These amounts are taxable to the children. They should be invested in an account of the child, so that resulting investment earnings are taxed in the hands of the child rather than the surviving adult. This is a legitimate way to avoid the Attribution Rules. (Only children 18 and over will receive a T4A(P) Slip.)

And, should you become permanently disabled, a CPP Disability Benefit may be payable to you and your minor dependent children. If you are not already doing so, you should try to maximize your contributions while you are employed or self-employed, to enhance CPP benefits payable to you when you need them.

171 TAXABLE RRSP WITHDRAWALS BEGIN AFTER AGE 69

After a lifetime of saving your pre-tax dollars, the time will one day come to make your RRSP withdrawals, as discussed below.

A taxpayer may withdraw funds from an RRSP at any time (provided individual investments in the plan can be liquidated). However, one *must* withdraw the funds after turning 69. Some tax sheltering can continue as the RRSP can be converted to a vehicle such as an annuity or RRIF.

The effect of these rules is that every year after turning 69 you will pay tax on at least a minimum amount of withdrawals from accumulations in your registered accounts or annuities. It can therefore pay to plan your income levels in advance of this deadline.

A taxpayer, for example, may contribute to an RRSP in each year in which there is unused RRSP contribution room from prior years, up until the end of the year in which he or she turns 69.

If over age 69, you can still contribute to an RRSP if you have the required contribution room, but then only to a spousal RRSP, provided that your spouse is under that age limit. In such cases, you can write off the spousal contribution on your own return. Using these options, you might plan to offset retiring allowances, CPP Benefits and RRIF payments to optimize your lifetime RRSP accumulations.

172 WORK AROUND THE THREE-YEAR HOLDING RULES FOR SPOUSAL RRSPS

When you make an RRSP contribution to a Spousal Plan, the spouse will be able to report the withdrawals in the future, provided that the amounts remain in the plan for at least three years from the last spousal contribution.

These "three-year" rules will not apply in the year the contributor dies; where the withdrawal is made due to marriage breakdown at a time the taxpayer and spouse are living apart; where the taxpayers were non-residents of Canada; or where the amount was directly transferred to another RRSP, RRIF or annuity that cannot be commuted (paid out) for at least three years.

Special rules also apply where the spouse transfers the amounts in the Spousal RRSP into a RRIF. In such cases any amounts withdrawn over and above the minimum required withdrawal will be taxed in the contributor spouse's hands until the holding requirement is met. You may wish to plan your withdrawals around these provisions to minimize the family's tax burden.

173 CUSTOM DESIGN YOUR SYSTEMATIC RRSP WITHDRAWALS

Most pensioners seek tax deferrals, as pension income and investment income sources are not considered to be "earned income" for RRSP purposes, and are included in taxable income in the year received.

Therefore, unless you earn income from part-time employment, or a small business you might start out of your home, pay taxable child or spousal support or earn net rental income you might receive from a revenue property, your RRSP contribution room will cease for future years. You will also have to deal with making RRSP withdrawals in some cases.

It is important to note that both principal and interest from the RRSP will be subject to 100% income inclusion when you do withdraw, which could bump the taxation of your income into a new tax bracket. (See Tip 175.) It is therefore always preferable to plan withdrawals over a period of years.

Peter, aged 50, is single and has no dependants. He has accumulated $200,000 in his RRSP. He has a comfortable lifestyle due to a pension from his former company, investments and the fact that he has very few expenses. He knows that, upon his death, his RRSP will be deemed disposed of and added to his income, in which case about one-half of the accumulations will be paid to the government by way of taxes. He knows his tax bracket at death will be higher than his current rate.

Peter may therefore wish to plan for an orderly withdrawal of his RRSP accumulations now to generate tax at a lower rate today, which will minimize taxes payable over the balance of his lifetime and upon death. He may also wish to enhance his plans for charitable giving. (See below.) He should therefore speak to his financial planner about a custom-designed systematic withdrawal plan.

174 MAXIMIZE YOUR CHARITABLE DONATIONS WITH RRSP INCOME

The earlier you plan your RRSP withdrawals, the more opportunity you will have for tax savings.

If you know you won't need the money, and you will have no surviving family member to leave it to, consider making withdrawals to maximize amounts you can give to charity. Deductible charitable donations are limited to 75% of your net income, with any restricted portion over and above this carried forward for five years. In addition, 25% of any taxable capital gains resulting from the gifts of capital property plus 25% of any recapture of depreciation included as income as a result of making such gifts will be added to the net income limitation.

Also, donations of certain publicly traded shares will now qualify for a reduced income inclusion rate of 37.5% upon their deemed disposition to the charity, if these donations were made after February 18, 1997 and before the year 2002. You may wish to speak to your financial advisor about this.

In the year you die and the year immediately preceding, charitable donations claims may be as high as 100% of your net income. Your executors may choose to deduct excess donations in the year of death or the immediately preceding year, or both.

You might, therefore, plan your RRSP withdrawals to achieve net income levels that allow you to maximize your charitable donations over a period of years, particularly if you have no heirs.

175 KNOW THE IMMEDIATE COST OF RRSP WITHDRAWAL

The object behind an RRSP is to contribute to it when your tax bracket is high and withdraw from it when you are in a lower one. This strategy will reduce the tax burden you face every tax season.

Many taxpayers are surprised that it costs them money immediately to access their RRSP accumulations. When you withdraw money from your RRSP tax will be withheld: 10% if the amount is $5,000 or less; 20% between $5,001 and $15,000; and 30% if you withdraw more than $15,000. Plan for this if you are using the fund for a specific purpose.

An "unmatured" RRSP (that is, one that is not yet paying you a retirement income), must be withdrawn or transferred into either an annuity or a Registered Retirement Income Fund (RRIF) before the end of the year in which you turn age 69. If you transfer amounts directly from an RRSP to an annuity or RRIF you can arrange for periodic income from the plan, which is taxed in the year received.

You can "mature" an RRSP at any time before you yourself reach the magic maturity age. Or you can simply withdraw lump sums, at your option, as renewal terms come up. You should plan renewal terms to minimize your tax liability, by knowing and understanding your marginal tax bracket. (See Tip 3.)

176 PLAN TO NAME YOUR SPOUSE AS THE BENEFICIARY OF YOUR RRSP

The fair market value of your RRSP must be included in your income in the year of death; however, a tax-free transfer of the RRSP accumulations is allowed if your spouse or common-law spouse is named as the beneficiary. That is, your spouse can choose to "roll over" the RRSP into his or her own RRSP.

If your spouse is not the beneficiary of the RRSP specifically, but is the beneficiary of the estate, the legal representative can elect with the spouse to treat the amounts as a "refund of premiums" payable to your spouse. These amounts will be deemed received by your spouse in the same calendar year they were paid to the estate, with the result that an RRSP again may be transferred to the spouse's RRSP. A special form must be filed in this case (T2019).

If there is no surviving spouse, but financially dependent children or grandchildren, amounts from your RRSP may be treated as a "refund of premiums" that are transferable to the dependant's RRSP, or annuity, depending on whether or not the child is infirm. Those children who are not infirm can only buy a term annuity. Speak to your tax advisor if this is a concern for you.

177 MANAGE YOUR PERSONAL RESIDENCES IN THE PRE-RETIREMENT PERIOD

It is not uncommon to own several real properties in your middle age: a summer cottage, a home in the Sunbelt, and perhaps a condo in the city for the "in between" months, or a revenue property that is inhabited only by tenants.

Provided that the rental income received is at fair market value, reported in Canadian funds, and a profit motive exists, you may be able to deduct from other income of the year any rental loss incurred. Where it is clear the intent of the purchase or change in use of the property was income-producing rather than personal use, subsequent gains on disposition would be taxable.

You should also enquire about gift and death taxes in the Sunbelt. These foreign tax implications could affect your decision to buy or rent a vacation property.

Also, be very careful not to compromise the tax-exempt status of one principal residence per family unit. At tax time, ask your tax advisor to help you define, on an annual basis, your tax-exempt principal residence, as described in Tip 178.

178 PRESERVE PRINCIPAL RESIDENCE STATUS ON VACATION PROPERTIES

If you only receive a small or incidental amount of income from your vacation property, it is not considered to be owned for the purposes of earning income and, therefore, could be considered to be your tax-exempt principal residence as long as you "ordinarily inhabited" the property at some time during the year.

Where there are two family residences, the principal residence designation can be made on an annual basis. The taxpayer can choose which property to claim for the taxable status on disposition, depending on which appreciated more during the time it was "ordinarily inhabited" by the taxpayer.

179 KEEP YOUR PROPERTY VALUES UPDATED

To help you decide whether to sell or transfer your residences, or if you are considering a change of use in your properties, be sure you have an updated valuation of your assets at hand. Use this checklist to do so.

❑ Prepare a list describing each property owned.

❑ Accumulate the following data to use in calculating any tax exempt portion for time the property was used as a personal residence:

   1. Number of years owned after 1971,
   2. Number of years owned after 1981,
   3. Amount of Capital Gains Election and ineligible portion of elected gain. (From your 1994 tax return.)

❑ Use of Property for each year owned:

   1. Personal enjoyment: from _____ to _____
   2. Rental income: from _____ to _____
   3. Business income: from _____ to _____

❑ Valuation of Property (attach supporting documentation):

   1. On acquisition: _____
   2. On change of use: _____
   3. Cost of major additions: _____
   4. As at December 31, 1971: _____
   5. As at December 31, 1981: _____
   6. As at February 22, 1994: _____
   7. On disposition: _____

❑ Ownership Details: List the properties owned by each spouse, breaking out those that have been transferred without consideration and those that are owned by the spouse in his or her own right.

180 CAPITAL COST ALLOWANCE CAN REDUCE INCOME TO NIL

If your property is an income-producing property, Capital Cost Allowance may be claimed on the building and other assets, based on acquisition costs and the costs of any additions or improvements. Remember that if Capital Cost Allowance is claimed on a building you inhabit, you automatically forfeit any principal residence status for the "business portion" of the residence. As well, the CCA deduction cannot create or increase a rental loss under any circumstances. CCA rates and classes for buildings are the following:

Buildings acquired after 1987:	Class 1:	4%
Buildings acquired before 1988:	Class 3:	5%
Furniture and Fixtures:	Class 8:	20%

In the year of acquisition, be sure to separate the value of the building from the value of the land, as land cannot be depreciated. One way to do this is to request the property tax assessment notice, which will break out these costs according to the city assessment. Also, be sure to add on the cost of legal fees paid on acquisition to the total cost before the proration for CCA purposes.

181 SCHEDULE BUILDINGS COSTING $50,000 OR MORE SEPARATELY

If you own several rental properties, there are special tax filing rules to observe. Every building costing $50,000 or more must be placed in a separate Class for depreciation purposes, except if two or more condo units are owned in the same building, in which case the condos are considered part of the same building.

As well, the half-year rule applies to all buildings acquired: in the year of acquisition, only one-half the usual CCA rate can be claimed. Be prepared to provide your tax advisor with the appropriate information.

182 KNOW WHETHER TO EXPENSE OR CAPITALIZE RENTAL COSTS

The most expensive error a taxpayer can make in reporting rental income and expenses is to write off in full expenditures that are obviously capital (depreciable) in nature. Ask the following questions to make the correct determination:

1. Does the expense extend the useful life of the property? If yes, it is generally considered a capital expenditure.

2. Does the expense recur after a short period of time? If so, it is probably a fully deductible operating expense.
3. Does the expense restore the property to its original condition? If so, it is probably a current expense, especially if the amounts are under $200.
4. Does the expenditure improve upon the original condition of the property? If yes, capitalize the item.

183 CLAIM YOUR AUTOMOBILE EXPENSES IF YOU MAINTAIN PROPERTIES

Revenue Canada has specific rules for the claiming of auto expenses against rental income. Auto expenses are generally only deductible if *two or more properties* are owned. Taxpayers with only one rental property may deduct auto costs for maintenance and repair work personally performed on the property by the owner, but only if the property is situated near the owner's residence.

Therefore, if you have an owner who rents his property because he lives or works 300 kilometres away, car trips for maintenance and repairs will not be allowed.

184 OFFICE-IN-HOME CLAIM MAY BE MADE AGAINST RENTAL INCOME

If the property owner uses a home office space for bookkeeping, placing ads, interviewing prospective tenants, meeting tenants for lease negotiations, etc., a claim may be made based on business use of operating expenses, the extent of the operations, the time involved using the office, etc. Revenue Canada would likely consider a single property operation insufficient to warrant a home office claim. However, office stationery expenses would be deductible in that case.

185 KNOW ABOUT OTHER TAX-DEDUCTIBLE EXPENSES FOR RENTAL PROPERTY OWNERS

Save receipts for the following tax-deductible expenditures and claim them on your tax return, if you own a rental property:
• accounting fees
• advertising
• commissions paid to leasing agents
• finder's fees paid in arranging a loan or mortgage. (The expense is deductible in equal portions over five years, unless it is paid

sooner. In that case, the balance of the expense is deductible in the year the mortgage is repaid.)

- insurance premiums for current year insurance coverage
- interest on money borrowed to purchase or improve your property, or interest paid to tenants on their rental deposits
- landscaping costs
- lease cancellation payments (amortize these over the remaining life of the lease to a maximum of 40 years)
- maintenance, repairs and utilities
- office in the home (more than one property) and stationery costs
- property taxes
- salary paid to those who supervise the properties.

186 FOREIGN EXCHANGE CAN INCREASE OR DECREASE YOUR INCOME

Canadian residents must report "world income" in Canadian funds on their tax returns.

If money you receive from a foreign source can be classified as "income" in nature (i.e., rental income), then any gains resulting from foreign exchange is considered to be taxable income to you.

However, if the gain in foreign exchange results from a "capital" transaction (i.e., when you sell the property itself and incur a capital gain), foreign exchange gains or losses are treated as capital gains or losses.

A $200 exemption is allowed for foreign currency gains on certain capital transactions.

Canadians who receive foreign rental income from their Sunbelt properties should also check into special elections to reduce foreign withholding taxes. Several countries (including Canada) allow non-resident property owners to base withholding taxes on net rather than gross rental income.

Also remember that a foreign tax credit can be claimed on the Canadian return to offset foreign taxes paid in another jurisdiction.

187 KNOW THE TAX RULES BEHIND DISPOSITION OF PRINCIPAL RESIDENCES

The exempt principal residence status of your home can change if you start using it for income-producing purposes (i.e., for rental or business purposes).

Whenever there is a change in use, there is a deemed disposition at fair market value and an immediate reacquisition at the same fair market value. Any gain on such a disposition is reduced by each year the property was designated to be a principal residence. If the home was your principal residence every year before you changed its use, no tax is due on any resulting capital gain until the property is actually sold.

You might also convert an income-producing property to a principal residence. Again, a deemed disposition is considered to have occurred at fair market value, and a special election can be made to defer the gain, as described below.

188 DEFER CAPITAL GAINS WITH SPECIAL ELECTIONS

You can elect to defer a capital gain on a principal residence if you move out of it and rent it. Under Section 45(2) of the Income Tax Act, you can elect to have the property remain your principal residence throughout the time it is rented, as long as you report your rental income and allowable expenses, and do not claim any capital cost allowance on the home.

The election will stay in effect until you dispose of the property or cancel the election. The property can be designated to be your principal residence for up to four years during the election period. Extensions of the four-year limitation are available in some instances.

If you change your rental property to a principal residence, an election under Section 45(3) of the Act will allow you to defer any capital gain on the deemed disposition until the home is actually sold. This election will not apply to any recaptured depreciation stemming from the change in use.

189 THE CONTROVERSIAL SENIORS BENEFIT HAS BEEN SCRAPPED

The March 6, 1996, federal budget introduced the proposed new Seniors Benefit, a plan to replace the Old Age Security, which is currently paid on a universal but income-tested and taxable basis, with an income-tested government pension that will be received tax-free by qualifying taxpayers. The new system was proposed to begin for most seniors in 2001, and its accelerated clawback structure made middle-income earners feel under attack.

Fortunately, the federal government decided to scrap this plan in July of 1998. Canadians can now expect, in the foreseeable future at any rate, a continuation of the current Old Age Security and Guaranteed Income Supplement benefits.

❊ 190 REPORTING RULES FOR U.S. SOCIAL SECURITY CHANGE

In recent years Canadian residents receiving U.S. Social Security benefits have seen numerous tax-reporting changes.

In the 1996 and 1997 tax filing year, Revenue Canada required that the full amount of U.S. Social Security pension received must be included as income on the Canadian tax return, in Canadian funds, even though recipients were subject to a withholding tax in the United States. Then a deduction for the full amount of the income reported was made on Line 256, rendering the pension almost fully tax exempt. Because the income inclusion increased net income, this transaction had the effect of reducing refundable and non-refundable tax credits.

Complaints by lower-income earners caused Canada and the U.S. to consider changes to the tax treatment of U.S. Social Security income in Canada. These latest changes, however, will be less advantageous to higher-income earners.

Under the latest rules, Canadian recipients will receive 100% of their U.S. Social Security from the United States. While the full amount of these benefits will be included in income on the Canadian return (in Canadian funds, of course), there will be an offsetting deduction on Line 256 of only 15%. These procedures will be in effect for the 1998 and future tax-filing years.

The 1996 and 1997 tax returns will be automatically reassessed by Revenue Canada, to provide refunds of any overpayments of withholding taxes kept in those years by the U.S. government. Also note that Canadians who emigrate must now file a special tax form (T1 Old Age Security Return) and report their world income in order to continue to receive their CPP and OAS abroad.

191 CHECK TAX TREATIES FOR FOREIGN PENSION EXEMPTIONS

Other foreign pension income sources have different tax treatment. For example, British pensions are fully taxable.

However, in the case of certain German pensions, the full amount received is reported on line 115 of the return; then an offsetting deduction is taken at Line 256. Again, convert the income to Canadian funds. The result is that these foreign pensions will increase net income but not taxable income.

It's therefore best to check the individual tax treaties we have with over 60 nations to clarify tax withholding and reporting exemptions.

CHAPTER 9

ENJOY YOUR TAX-WISE RETIREMENT

Do you know...

* *You can minimize taxable income in retirement...*
* *You can manage your quarterly tax instalments to increase cash flow...*
* *You can split the reporting of CPP benefits received between spouses...*
* *You can decrease your OAS Clawback in hardship cases...*
* *The new Refundable Medical Expense Supplement can help you pay for expensive medications...*
* *The new Caregivers' Tax Credit can provide financial relief in troubled times...*

Retirement. For many this is a period of adjustment and change, both personally and financially. It can be a new beginning of promise and self-actualization. It can also bring with it the physical and financial challenges of aging.

Not surprisingly, there are also significant income tax consequences. Take Harold, for example, who recently retired from a career as a real estate agent. He looked up and smiled when his first Old Age Security cheque appeared in the mailbox. "First steady income I've ever had!" he smirked.

The milestone of turning 65 brings with it a whole new tax-filing profile...new income sources, new tax brackets, new tax credits. It's important to get it all straight, and then to plan to minimize tax under the new circumstances.

For example, those taxpayers who turned 65 during the tax year will start receiving OAS benefits. They want to stay on the right side of two income thresholds: the $25,921 net income threshold used for the purposes of claiming the Age Amount, and the $53,215 net income threshold, used to clawback OAS benefits themselves.

Couples receiving CPP benefits will want to split them, if there is one high- and one low-income earner in the family.

Those receiving superannuation and those who receive a periodic pension from a RRIF or other annuity based on RRSP deposits, either because they are over 65 or receiving the amounts as a result of a spouse's death, will be allowed to claim a $1000 pension income amount.

There are several other issues facing retirees: minimization of quarterly instalment payments to be made to Revenue Canada during the year, the proper reporting of medical expenses, the claiming of provisions for the sick and disabled, the orderly withdrawal of RRSP and RRIF deposits.

One of the most stressful aspects of living on a fixed income is dealing with the uncontrollables: the highs and lows in the marketplace, for example, at a time when risk-taking must be minimized. One must preserve capital while drawing income. Together with very low interest rates, high taxation, and recent low dollar values, seniors can and do feel a crimp in their lifestyle.

So let's begin with the first challenge: understanding the tax implications of the senior's profile.

192 LEARN TO ANTICIPATE QUARTERLY INSTALMENT REMITTANCE REQUIREMENTS

One of the major changes in cash flow planning for seniors is the responsibility they have to remit their own tax instalment payments. The government requires prepayments of tax on taxable income for the current tax year under three options:

1. Payments according to Revenue Canada's billing notices (no interest is charged if there is a shortfall at April 30).
2. Payments based on the prior year tax liability only (interest will be charged if there is a balance due at April 30).
3. Payments based on an estimate of current year tax liability (interest will be charged again if there is a shortfall on April 30).

Because of this prepayment requirement, which is based on each individual's tax liability, it is important to plan RRSP and RRIF withdrawals, adjust withholding tax on private pensions, understand the tax reporting for receipt of interest payments, and how to split income with your spouse, in order to avoid or reduce the payment of the quarterly tax instalment amounts.

193 STAY UNDER THE $2,000 INSTALMENT PAYMENT THRESHOLD

Those who do not have any, or enough, tax remitted at source will be required to remit income taxes by instalment four times each year: March 15, June 15, September 15 and December 15. (Farmers may continue to remit once a year on December 31.)

Information from the immediately prior year tax return and the two preceding tax years will be used to determine whether an individual will be required to make quarterly instalment payments. You will be required to remit to the federal government if the difference between tax payable and amounts withheld at source is greater than $2,000 in both the current year and either of the two preceding years.

The tax payable will include both the combined federal and provincial income taxes. Late or deficient instalment payments will be subject to an interest penalty, which amounts to the rate charged on treasury bills of the last quarter, plus 4%. Be sure your tax-withholding arrangements keep you out of the instalment profile, or be prepared to prepay your taxes on a quarterly basis.

194 DECREASE INSTALMENT PAYMENTS AND INCREASE CASH FLOW

It's a good idea not to overpay your instalment remittances when you could be investing or otherwise using your precious resources.

Many seniors don't know that they can request that your instalment payment billings be reduced if income clearly will be below that of the previous tax year. This could happen if you will be applying capital losses to capital gains this year, or if your income otherwise decreased over the previous years. Or, you can plan to reduce your same-level income with some new tax planning decisions: like making a Spousal RRSP contribution, if possible, or by splitting Canada Pension Plan benefits with your spouse.

To lessen your burden at tax time, you can also request that more tax be withheld from your monthly Old Age Security, Canada Pension Plan, or private pension cheque. However, this option will reduce your monthly cash flow, which could be a problem for some.

You might also consider changing your asset mix; that is, the type of assets held in your non-registered investment accounts. As you know, the accrued gains in equity-based investments are not taxed until disposition. Also, dividends and capital gains income is taxed at lower marginal tax rates than pensions and interest. Therefore, it is possible to preserve your capital by managing your investments in such a way as to reduce the quarterly withdrawal of funds used to prepay your taxes. Speak to your tax and investment advisor about this.

195 OFFSET INTEREST CHARGES BY PREPAYING YOUR INSTALMENTS

Winter travellers may offset Revenue Canada interest charges on instalment remittances by prepaying their instalments before they leave. Alternatively, Revenue Canada can be given the required payments in post-dated cheques. If you mistakenly underpay your instalments, you can avoid interest charges by overpaying your next instalment to offset the deficiency.

Should your investment and other income sources drop due to economic conditions, you may request that a change be made to your current remittance method to an estimate of taxes payable for the current year, so that you can reduce your instalment remittance requirements altogether.

This is a good reason to monitor your income level throughout the year so as to minimize the amount you must prepay to the tax department.

196 COMPUTE YOUR AGE AMOUNT AT 65

At the age of 65 taxpayers will calculate whether they are eligible to claim a new non-refundable tax credit: the Age Amount. This may be claimable if the taxpayer reached age 65 during the year, and has income within certain thresholds. The Age Amount is a maximum non-refundable tax credit of $3,482.

However, there is a wrinkle you should be aware of. If you earn more than $25,921 in "net income" from pensions, investments or other sources, the Age Amount you would otherwise be entitled to will be reduced by 15% of any income over $25,921, to a maximum of $3,482, starting in 1995 and subsequent years.

When you factor in provincial taxes, this new tax provision could cost you up to 27% of the Age Amount or up to approximately $940 more, if your income wipes out the Age Credit completely. In addition, the restriction and its resulting tax liability could affect how much you'll pay on your quarterly tax instalment plan. Therefore it is important to prepare some preliminary tax calculations before year end, to see just how you will be affected by the Age Amount Restriction.

In the case of married couples, the higher-income earner can transfer the Age Amount of the spouse to his or her own tax return by using Schedule 2, if the lower-income earner does not need all of the credits to reduce taxes payable. This is a lucrative figure that can save you hundreds of dollars.

When one spouse dies, the OAS for that person stops. Also, in the year of death, the Age Amount is not allowed unless the taxpayer reached age 65 before the date of death. It is therefore important to plan for the potential changes in your tax-filing profile due to the loss of one spouse.

197 UNDUE HARDSHIP MAY AFFECT YOUR OAS INCOME

Old Age Security pension payments (OAS) are received by those who turn age 65 during the year and are reported as taxable income and subject to a "Clawback" calculation. Each individual, whose net income exceeds $53,215, will have a withholding tax applied to Old Age Security cheques starting in July each year, based on income reported on the immediately prior tax year.

Every tax filing year, the clawback tax withheld will be credited to the liabilities otherwise payable and the new clawback will be prepared. It is therefore important to arrange your tax affairs so as to report the lowest net income possible at tax time, in order to have a direct affect on your monthly income from the OAS during the next year.*

Canadian residents will continue to receive their OAS cheques even if no tax return has been filed, unless they have ignored a Demand to File by the Minister, in which case the payments will stop. Non-residents are not as lucky. If they fail to file their prescribed form, the OAS will not be forwarded.

Revenue Canada may ignore the withholding tax on OAS if you can successfully plead undue hardship. This may happen, for example, if your income decreases sharply between the base tax year and the year of receipt. In such cases, contact your Tax Services Office to apply for tax relief.

---

*Starting in 1998, net income for OAS purposes will be adjusted to provide a deduction for employment expenses, CPP and EI premiums, and for some taxpayers a break on reporting grossed-up income.

198 SPLIT THE CPP BENEFITS BETWEEN SPOUSES

One way to avoid clawbacks and reduce instalment tax payments is to split income sources between the two spouses. Many taxpayers are unaware that effective January 1, 1987, rights to Canada Pension Plan retirement benefits may be assigned to a spouse, including a common-law spouse. This is an excellent way of splitting the reporting of the CPP retirement income between spouses. For the purpose of income splitting, the benefits must be retirement benefits, and either a single or double assignment of benefits may be made.

Under a single assignment, only one spouse has applied for or is receiving the CPP retirement benefits. The other spouse will not have previously made CPP contributions, and must be at least 60 years of age. The result of assignment is that part of the pension received by the contributor is paid to, and therefore reported by, each spouse on the tax return.

Under a double assignment, both spouses will be eligible to receive or are receiving CPP retirement benefits, but total benefits received by both will be distributed evenly. Total pensions payable to each individual will be split; that is, it is not possible to split only one spouse's CPP retirement pension. The amount that is split between spouses is calculated as 50% of the number of months in the marriage, divided by the number of months in the contributory period (starting from age 18 or January 1966). Retirement benefits from CPP do not qualify as "earned income for RRSP purposes." Work out your returns both ways — with the CPP Spousal Split and without it — to determine the best tax position.

Also remember that, in the year a taxpayer starts receiving benefits from CPP, there is no longer a requirement to contribute premiums to the plan through employment or self-employment. Therefore, any CPP premium amounts paid after the month in which the taxpayer starts to collect CPP benefits, will result in an overpayment, which can be applied for when you file your tax return. This usually results in an extra tax refund. This same rule holds true in the year of death, when premiums need only be paid up to the date of death, or in the year *a taxpayer turns 70,* when no premiums are required after this month.

199 CREATE RRSP ROOM WITH CPP DISABILITY BENEFITS

Effective on amounts received after 1990, CPP disability benefits have qualified and will continue to qualify as earned income for RRSP purposes.

This means that 18% of the CPP disability benefits received in the prior year can be contributed to an RRSP and used to reduce your tax liability, provided you are not restricted from doing so because of your age.

200 SPLIT THE REPORTING OF CPP LUMP SUM PAYMENTS

It is quite common for a taxpayer to have to wait months, and often years, to receive a CPP disability amount, with the result that a retroactive lump sum can be received in one tax year. The part of the benefit that relates to years other than the current tax year is automatically applied to the prior years by Revenue Canada if it exceeds $300.

Report the full amount on the T4A(P) on the current year's tax return. Revenue Canada will then adjust the return. When the true net income of the recipient of the CPP disability pension is known, go back to adjust the spouse's return for a possible Spousal Amount, medical expenses, charitable donations or political contributions transfer, if these changes give the family unit a better tax benefit.

201 KNOW WHAT INCOME QUALIFIES FOR THE PENSION INCOME AMOUNT

The $1,000 pension income amount on Line 314 of the tax return is available to certain taxpayers, depending on age and source of pension income received. The rules for claiming it are as follows:

If the taxpayer is over age 64 and in receipt of the following, the $1,000 pension income amount applies to offset:

(a) pension payments received from a superannuation pension plan as part of a life annuity;

(b) annuity payments from a Registered Retirement Income Fund/RSP;

(c) annuity payments from a Deferred Profit Sharing Plan;

(d) taxable portion of other annuities, including earnings from foreign sources, less any amount deducted at Line 256;

(e) annuity payments from an Income Averaging Annuity Contract (IAAC);

(f) income from a U.S. IRA included on Line 115.

If the taxpayer is under age 65, the $1,000 pension income amount also applies to offset the following income sources:

• pension payments received from a pension plan as a life annuity, less any amounts transferred to a spousal RRSP

- amounts listed in (b) to (f) above if received as a result of the spouse's death.

Ineligible pension income sources for the $1,000 pension credit include:

- Old Age Security and Supplements
- Spouse's Allowances
- Canada Pension Plan benefits
- Retirement Compensation Arrangements
- employment benefit plans
- employee trust or prescribed provincial pension plans (Saskatchewan Pension Plan)
- death benefits
- lump-sum payments on withdrawal of a pension fund
- Deferred Profit Sharing Plan or Registered Pension Plan payments transferred to an RRSP
- retiring allowances such as severance pay
- salary deferral arrangements.

Remember that pension amounts may be transferred to the higher-income spouse.

BONUS TIPS FOR THOSE IN NEED

 ## 202 DON'T FORGET TO CLAIM YOUR MEDICAL EXPENSES

One of the most lucrative yet most commonly missed tax credits for uninsured taxpayers is the medical expenses credit, its partner, the Refundable Medical Expense Supplement, as well as its two associates, the Disability Tax Credit and the Caregivers' Tax Credit.

First, it is important for those who pay any amounts towards medical expenses or health insurance plans to claim medical expenses on the tax return as a non-refundable tax credit. This includes the expenses of the taxpayer or spouse and dependants for any 12-month period ending in the tax year that is in excess of 3% of net income. (The 3% limitation has been restricted to a maximum of $1,614 since 1992.) Because of this restriction, it is usually more effective to claim the medical expenses on the tax return of the person with the lower net income. This is particularly important with the introduction of the Refundable Medical Expenses Supplement in 1997 and future years. In the case of a deceased taxpayer, expenses may be included for any 24-month period including the date of death.

Medical expenses are not restricted to those incurred or paid in Canada, but they must have been paid on behalf of a Canadian resident or deemed resident. Starting in 1996, supporting individuals only claim the medical expense tax credit for qualifying expenses incurred on behalf of a dependent spouse, child, grandchild, parent, grandparent, brother, sister, uncle, aunt, niece, or nephew. In addition, starting in 1997, up to $10,000 in full or part-time home attendant care costs for those with a prolonged mental or physical impairment may be claimed as a medical expense. In the year of death, this amount increases to $20,000. And in 1998 new qualifying claims include expenses for costs of special training for those who care for a disabled dependant.

Be sure to file for your medical expenses on the T1 General return, but reduce them by any reimbursements received from health insurance plans. You can also go back and recover missed credits of prior years by requesting an adjustment to your prior tax returns all the way back to 1985 and submitting receipts.

203 LIST ALL MEDICAL EXPENDITURES THAT ARE TAX DEDUCTIBLE

One of the most commonly missed medical expenses is Blue Cross or other private health care plan premiums. The following list of expenses gives other common items often missed on the tax return:

Type of Expense	Description
Medical Practitioner	Dentists, doctors, nurses, osteopaths, chiropractors, naturopaths, therapists, podiatrists, optometrists, psychiatrists, psychologists, speech therapists, Christian Science practitioners.
Payments to Societies	Physiotherapists employed by Arthritis Society and Associations, Victorian Order of Nurses, Canadian Mothercraft Society.
Private Hospitals	Possession of municipal licence designating institution as a hospital is necessary. Respite care costs of up to $5,000 will be deductible as well.
Attendants	For full-time care of person in nursing home; care in a self-contained domestic establishment; accompanying patient in travelling for medical treatment (costs of board and lodging).
Institutions	Costs for care and/or training of physically or mentally disabled person, including persons suffering from behavioural problems and attendance problems. Rehabilitative therapy, including training in sign language and lip reading are also allowed beginning in 1992 and for future years.

Services	Payments for sign language interpretation provided to someone who has a speech or hearing impairment, if the fees are paid to a person engaged in the business of providing such services; reasonable moving expenses (up to a maximum of $2,000) of an individual who lacks normal physical development or who has a severe and prolonged mobility impairment, to a place that is more accessible; reasonable costs of alteration to the driveway of an individual's residence in order to facilitate access to a bus; amounts that are not in excess of $5,000 and/or equal to 20% of the cost of a van that has been adapted for a person who uses a wheelchair at the time of purchase or within 6 months of purchase.
Transportation and Travel Costs	By ambulance for a patient, paid to a person who is employed in providing such transportation services; costs for use of vehicle (land, air or water) owned by taxpayer or family member as well as other expenses of transporting one accompanying individual if the patient is certified to require an attendant. Such reasonable travel expenses are allowed only if patient and attendant must travel 80 km or more to receive medical services not available in locality; also allowed if patient travels alone; reasonable expenses must be verified by receipts.

204 CALCULATE THE REFUNDABLE MEDICAL EXPENSE SUPPLEMENT

Starting with the 1997 tax-filing year, a new refundable medical expense supplement is available to those individuals whose "adjusted" income meets certain thresholds. The eligible individual is someone who is 18 years of age or older at the end of the year and whose total business and employment income (excluding disability benefits) is at least $2,500. This "adjusted income" figure is also defined as being the income of the individual and that of his/her spouse.

The credit is equal to the lesser of $500 and 25% of the medical expense credit claimed elsewhere on the tax return for the year. This supplement is then reduced by 5% of the net family income over $16,069. It is eliminated when net family income exceeds $26,069. These amounts will be indexed in future years.

Therefore, to maximize your claim under this new provision it is important to include all medical expenses incurred, to choose the best 12-month period ending in the tax year to maximize your claim (you might be able to reach back and include some unclaimed expenses from last year) and then to claim these amounts on the return of the person with the lower net income to benefit the most from the 3% net income limitation, and this new refundable tax credit.

205 THE NEW CAREGIVERS' TAX CREDIT

For the 1998 and subsequent tax years, a new non-refundable tax credit will be available for individuals who care for their sick and disabled relatives. It is available in two specific instances:

1. If the in-home care is provided for the individual's child, grandchild, parent, grandparent, sibling, uncle, aunt, niece or nephew or if the person is an adult who is dependent on the individual due to a physical or mental infirmity, and is at least 18 years of age.
2. If in-home care is provided for parents or grandparents who are age 65 before the end of the tax year and who are dependent because of physical or mental infirmity.

The maximum amount of this new credit is $2,353. This will be received in full if the dependant's net income does not exceed $11,500. If the dependant's net income is more than $11,500 but less than $13,853, then the credit will be reduced by 17% of the amount by which the dependant's net income exceeds $11,500.

No credit will be available if the dependant's net income exceeds $13,853, or if a dependant tax credit has been claimed in respect of that dependant by any person. Equivalent-to-Spouse claims will reduce this amount.

Example: A taxpayer's 90-year-old grandmother lives with the taxpayer and his/her family. The grandmother has net income of $12,500.

Basic Credit		$ 2,353 (a)
Reduction of Credit:		
Dependant's net income	$12,500 (i)	
Less base amount	$11,500 (ii)	
Subtotal (i-ii)		$ 1,000 (b)
Caregiver Tax Credit (a-b)		**$ 1,353**

206 BE AWARE OF DISABILITY CREDIT ELIGIBILITY CRITERIA

Those who suffer from a severe and prolonged medical impairment may claim a special tax credit on the tax return, or if not taxable, may transfer it to their supporting individuals. To qualify, a doctor must verify the nature of the infirmity following strict guidelines set out by Revenue Canada.

A prolonged impairment is one that has lasted for at least 12 continuous months ending in the tax year or has begun in the tax year and is expected to last at least 12 continuous months. A severe impairment is one that, on a prolonged basis, markedly restricts all or substantially all of the time (90% or more) a person's ability to perform basic activities of daily living.

A marked restriction is one that causes the person to be unable to perform basic activities of daily living even with the use of appropriate devices, medication or therapy or causes the person to take an excessive amount of time to perform basic activities of daily living. Persons with permanent visual impairment (legal blindness) qualify for the tax credit.

In the case of children with disabilities, the child's developmental progress in relation to the norm and the prognosis of the condition as it affects the child's ability to perform basic activities of daily living are taken into consideration.

Basic activities of daily living are defined as (a) feeding and dressing oneself; (b) eliminating (bowel and bladder functions); (c) walking; (d) speaking, so as to be understood by a person who knows him in a quiet setting; (e) hearing, so that the person can understand a conversation with a familiar person in a quiet setting; (f) cognitive functions (perceiving, thinking and remembering).

For the purposes of claiming this credit, basic activities of daily living do not include working, recreation, housekeeping or social activities.

Obtain Form T2201 Disability Credit Certificate, and have your doctor sign it. This credit may be claimed by a supporting individual for severely disabled dependent grandchildren, parents, and grandparents starting in the 1996 and future years, as well as for dependent children and spouses.

Note: Effective the 1998 and future tax years, occupational therapists and psychologists will be allowed to sign the Disability Certificate for the purposes of this credit.

207 FILE BACK TO RECOVER MISSED DISABILITY TAX CREDITS

Usually, the onset of a disability in the family is a stressful event. The tax consequences of the disability are often forgotten. Fortunately, the disability credit can be recovered by requesting an adjustment to a prior-filed return. If your loved one suffered from any of the following afflictions, you may still be able to claim this lucrative tax credit:

- legal blindness (20/200 or less) or severe macular degeneration

- mobility: confinement to a bed or wheelchair for a substantial part of the day or severe arthritis involving multiple major joints
- communication: profound bilateral deafness, expressive and sensory aphasia, speech impairment
- mental functions: supervision required in self-care activities including dressing, feeding, bathing and eating
- cardio-respiratory systems: dyspnea or angina while performing basic living activities
- neurological systems: severe epilepsy, severe ataxia, bowel or bladder incontinence, marked decrease in mentation, marked dysarthia
- genito-urinary system: persons disabled despite receiving peritonal dialysis; person with renal failure needing 23 or more hours a week of haemodialysis
- endocrine system: diabetes mellitus that causes peripheral vascular insufficiency
- multiple body systems: including pulmonary, gastrointestinal or central nervous systems
- cancer: related to the severity and effect of the cancer on ability to perform basic activities.

The credit ($4,233) is worth close to $1,200 each year. Recouping missed Disability Credits can go a long way in helping a family during difficult times.

208 TRANSFER ELIGIBLE TAX CREDITS BETWEEN SPOUSES

Four different provisions on the tax return may be transferred between spouses, including common-law spouses. They are:

- Pension Income Amount
- Age Amount
- Disability Amount
- Tuition and Education Amount (up to $5,000 in tuition fees and/ or education credits).

If your spouse is not taxable, or does not need all of the credits listed above to reduce income taxes to zero, transfer the unused portions of his or her tax credits to your return to reap bonus tax benefits. To do so, complete Schedule 2.

Be sure to revisit this credit in 1998, as the spouse will benefit from the new Personal Amount Supplement when computing this transfer.

209 GROUP TAX CREDITS ON ONE RETURN TO MAXIMIZE FAMILY TAX BENEFITS

As a general policy, Revenue Canada allows a husband and wife (including a common-law spouse) to group certain expenditures — medical expenses, charitable donations and political contributions — paid by each individual spouse on one tax return to maximize tax benefits.

For example, medical expenses should be combined and claimed on the return of the lower taxable income earner to maximize the 3% of net income limitation. Donations, on the other hand, should usually be grouped and claimed by the higher-income earner, to maximize the use of the 75% of net income limitation, effective the 1997 and future tax years.

Political contributions should also be grouped and claimed by the higher earner, up to a maximum contribution of $1,150 (which equals the $500 credit allowed).

Your goal is to file your returns in such a way as to pay the least amount of taxes possible as a family unit.

210 MAKE SURE IT'S DEDUCTIBLE

For dozens of tax tips for your home business, see *Make Sure It's Deductible*, a new book from Canada's bestselling tax author, Evelyn Jacks.

CONCLUSION

At The Jacks Institute, when we teach income tax preparation to Canadians across the country, we believe in what we call the "Best Benefit Theory":

> *"It is not good enough simply to compute the tax return mathematically correctly: be sure you have claimed all deductions, credits and tax planning benefits your family is entitled to."*

These tax tips are written to help you recognize tax savers when they arise in response to different circumstances in your life. I hope you have found them enlightening, that they will help you seek out qualified professional help when needed, and that they will ultimately save you and your family money.

Many happy returns,
Evelyn Jacks

CHAPTER 10

36 COMMON
TAX-FILING TRAPS

The following are common tax-filing traps you might fall into when you prepare your tax return. Watch out for them and save extra money!

INCOME REPORTING

1. *Missing T4 Slips:* In 1998 we have a brand new T4 Slip. Be sure to read it carefully, enter all appropriate information on the right lines and do not double report your income! This could happen with Taxable Benefits, which are already included in the Total Employment Income. Remember, even casual employment is taxable, as are tips and gratuities and employment for which no T4 Slip was received. In such cases, estimate income and source deductions, using your pay stubs. In the case of service industry employees, keep a daily log of all tips earned, to breeze through a tax audit.

2. *Missing Interest Income:* Financial institutions will not send out a T5 Slip if interest earnings are less than $50; so check bank books for this information. Don't forget to claim interest Revenue Canada may have paid you. Look for this on your Notice of Assessment.

3. *Double-Reported Interest:* If you have pre-reported interest on compounding investments such as Canada Savings Bonds or Guaranteed Investment Certificates, be sure to subtract any such amounts from the total income you receive in the year you cash the investment.

4. *Over-reported Capital Gains:* Those who previously made a Capital Gains Election in 1994 should be careful to use the new cost base information created by that election, once the actual disposition of the elected asset happens. Special rules apply to mutual fund holders.

5. *Over-Reported Scholarship Income:* Claim a $500 exemption on any income received during the year from scholarships, fellowships and bursaries. Students qualify for significant enhancements to the federal tax system in 1998, including increased education amounts and a new student loan interest credit.

6. *Over-Reported Alimony Income:* If you have received a lumpsum settlement on the occasion of your marital break-up, the amount is tax-free to the recipient and not deductible by the payor. And remember that for agreements negotiated or changed after April 30, 1997, child support will no longer be taxable to the recipient or tax deductible to the payor.

7. *Business Income Reporting Changes:* Once again in 1998, those businesses that switched their non-calendar fiscal year ends to December 31 in 1995, must be careful to compute income earned this year by taking into account the 10-year reserve provisions. Remember, a transitional reserve can be claimed to reduce the impact of the additional taxes generated by this one time adjustment. An alternative calculation is available to those who elected to retain their non-calendar fiscal year ends (see Form T1139).

8. *Over-reported Income From Social Benefits:* You will be required to report any amounts received from Social Assistance, Workers' Compensation or Federal Old Age Supplements on the tax return, even though these amounts are not taxable. The amounts will be used, however, to decrease refundable tax credits otherwise payable to you. Be sure to take the offsetting deduction for these amounts on Line 250.

9. *Report Foreign Holdings*: Canadians are required to report world income in Canadian funds. However, certain assets must now also be documented every year for Revenue Canada's records. For 1997 and future tax years, it will be necessary to disclose dealings with foreign trusts and affiliates, or face penalty provisions. It is proposed that for 1998 those with specified foreign investment properties valued over $100,000 at any time during the year will have to report these annually on Form T1135.

CLAIMING OF DEDUCTIONS

10. *Under-Utilized RRSP Contributions:* Maximize your allowable RRSP contribution room to reduce net income, which will in turn increase other provisions available, such as the federal and provincial Child Tax Benefits, the Goods and Services Tax Credit, the Refundable Medical Expense Supplement, and other provincial tax credits.

11. *Missed RPP Deductions:* Remember to carry forward and deduct any unused past service contributions made to a Registered Pension Plan in prior years. Missing these deductions is a common occurrence for government employees such as teachers.

12. *Under-Claimed Child Care Expenses:* While child care is usually claimed by the lower-income earner, the higher earner can take a limited deduction if the spouse was attending school full- or part-time at a designated educational institute, or was hospitalized or incarcerated for at least two weeks in the year. Obtain Form T778. Remember, for parents who both attend school there is a special new child care calculation for 1996 and future years.

13. *Under-Reported Moving Expenses:* Keep all receipts, then claim costs of all removal expenses for yourself and your family, provided you have moved at least 40 kilometres closer to a new work or self-employment location. These deductions include temporary living accommodations for up to 15 days at the new location, real estate commissions paid to sell the house at the old location and removal expenses for the household effects and family members. In 1998 even more deductions are available, including amounts paid for costs of keeping up an old residence for up to three months after the move to the new location. (See Tip 64.) However, to qualify there must be employment, self-employment or scholarship income at the new location.

14. *Missing Alimony or Maintenance Deductions:* Claim the periodic payments you make to your ex-spouse and children as per your written agreement, judgment or court order for the current year, and the immediately preceding year, if the agreement was made prior to May 1, 1997. (Agreements signed after this date render child support not taxable.) If you were a recipient of such payments, and were required to repay some or all of them, claim a deduction for any amounts previously included in income. Spousal support continues to be taxable to the recipient and deductible by the payor.

15. *Missed Carrying Charges:* Claim the costs of your Safety Deposit Box, investment accounting fees, and interest paid on investment loans (for qualifying non-registered investments including charges for purchasing Canada Savings Bonds on a payroll plan). But remember that the administration fees for your RRSP will no longer be tax deductible after 1995. RESP fees are no longer deductible after 1997.

16. *Unclaimed Employment Expenses:* Don't forget to claim auto, travel, cost of supplies or in the case of commission salespeople,

entertainment and promotion, if you are required by your contract of employment to pay these amounts out of your own pocket. Your employer must sign Form T2200 to verify that all required conditions are met in order for you to make this claim.

17. *Legal Expenses:* While you cannot claim the cost of your legal fees paid to obtain a divorce or separation, you can claim the costs of enforcing payments already established by the courts.

18. *Unclaimed Accounting Fees:* In general, accounting fees can only be used to offset income from business or property; however, accounting fees paid to fight an assessment from Revenue Canada will be tax deductible.

19. *Capital Gains Exemption:* Don't forget that the $500,000 Super Exemption is still with us and available to you should you sell qual-ified small business corporation shares or qualified farm property.

20. *Northern Residents' Deductions:* A special deduction may be made if you have lived in a "prescribed northern zone" or a "prescribed intermediate zone" for six consecutive months or more during the year. Obtain a copy of Revenue Canada's Northern Residents' Guide.

CLAIMING OF NON-REFUNDABLE TAX CREDITS

21. *The New Personal Amount Supplement:* Don't forget to claim this new credit for lower-income earners. For couples, a credit based on net family income is available.

22. *Restrictions on Claiming the Age Amount:* Since 1994, the Age Amount has been restricted in cases where net income exceeds $25,921. Be sure to make the calculation or you could owe Revenue Canada more after you file your return.

23. *Equivalent-to-Spouse Amount:* If you are a single parent, who is not living common law, and you are solely supporting your child, parent or grandparent, a non-refundable tax credit may be available to you, depending on the level of your dependant's income, calculated in the same manner as the Spousal Amount.

24. *The New Caregivers' Tax Credit:* Claim this credit if you are looking after an adult relative who is mentally or physically infirm.

25. *Over or Under-Contributions to the Canada Pension Plan:* It is possible if you had more than one employer, that you have over-contributed your CPP premiums. Or, if you turned 18, the age of 70, started to receive CPP retirement benefits, or in the year of

death, premiums are only required for a portion of the year. File Form T2204 with your tax return to make the calculations.

26. *Pension Income Amount:* Those who receive periodic pension payments from a company pension plan may claim a maximum of $1,000 under the pension income amount to offset net income, regardless of age. The credit is also allowed for annuity payments under certain plans such as a RRIF or other annuities if you are over age 65, or receiving the amounts as a result of your spouse's death.

27. *Tuition Fees:* If you are attending a designated post-secondary educational institute, including one certified by Human Resources Development Canada in providing occupational skills, a non-refundable tax credit is claimable if tuition exceeds $100, and the taxpayer is at least 16 years old. Tuition fees are claimable for amounts expended for sessions held during the calendar year only. Remember that you can now carry forward such amounts, if not needed to reduce taxable income or if there is no one to whom the amounts can be transferred.

28. *Education Credit:* Claim $200 a month for each month you were in full-time attendance at a designated educational institute during the calendar year, or starting in 1998, $60 a month for each month of part-time attendance. Those who can only attend part-time because of a disability may claim the full-time credit. Again the amounts may be carried forward to future years, if this is more advantageous to you.

29. *Transfer of Tuition/Education Amounts:* Transfer up to $5,000 of these two amounts to your supporting parent, grandparent, spouse, or legal guardian; but transfer only what's needed to reduce their income. The rest can be carried forward by the student.

30. *Claim the New Student Loan Interest Deduction:* This is available to those who pay interest on federal/provincial student loans.

31. *Claim All Medical Expenses:* Medical expenses such as Blue Cross or other private health insurance premiums are claimable for the best 12-month period ending in the tax year. Also be sure to claim glasses, dental work, hearing aids and their batteries, prescription drugs, and even travelling expenses for prescribed medical treatments not available in your home community. Receipts are required. Don't forget to use these medical claims in the computation of the Refundable Medical Expense Supplement available for the 1997 and future tax years.

32. *Couple-Up on Charities:* Revenue Canada will allow spouses to claim each other's charitable donations. It is better to do so on the return of the higher-income earner to maximize the two-tier credit structure.

You can also "save" the donations and group them for one claim in a period of up to five years, provided they are never claimed twice. Remember though, generally the claim may not exceed 75% of your net income in any one tax year, or 100% of net income in the year of death or the immediately preceding year.

SPECIAL PROVISIONS

33. *Political Contributions:* Significant political contribution credits of up to $500 may be claimed against federal taxes payable, and in some provinces, against provincial taxes.

34. *Labour-Sponsored Venture Capital Tax Credits:* A federal tax credit of up to $750 may be claimed for these RRSP-eligible investments. Many provinces also match this credit to be used to offset provincial taxes payable.

35. *GST/HST Rebate:* Be sure to make a claim for the GST/HST Rebate any time you claimed expenses from employment or a partnership in Line 212 or 229 of the tax return.

36. *Instalment Payments:* Don't forget to dig out documentation for the quarterly instalment payments you made during the year, to offset the taxes payable on your tax return.

CHAPTER 11

20 TIPS FOR YEAR END TAX PLANNING

1. *Know Your Tax-filing Rights:* Every Canadian has the right to arrange his or her affairs within the framework of the law so as to pay the least amount of income taxes possible. To identify and take advantage of all your options, set aside some time at year end to analyse your current year's income and expense records and your current financial portfolio. It could pay off at tax time.

2. *Determine Your Family's Tax-Filing Profile:* List all major financial and personal events that occurred in the current tax year to determine their tax consequences. Then, dig out last year's returns to see if you missed filing for a lucrative tax deduction or credit and to check out remaining RRSP room. If you still have not filed a prior year's return, doing so now could result in a nice tax refund in time for Christmas or, at very least, some extra RRSP contribution room.

3. *File Adjustments for Missed Tax Provisions:* When you've found prior errors, correct them by filing a letter with your Tax Services Office to claim your overpaid taxes or use the Revenue Canada Form T1ADJ. Every penny counts! You may go back to tax year 1985 to request changes for most provisions.

4. *List All Missing Information:* Do you wish to consult with your broker before year end? Give to your favourite charity? Claim home office expenses for the first time, order new forms from Revenue Canada? Get those new glasses or get that dental work done? Make a list of expenditures to plan to reduce taxes before year end. Gather the information for tax season, including a mortgage interest statement

from your financial institution, receipts for child care, moving or other expenses, as well as auto expense log books.

5. *Sort Medical Expenses Before Year End:* Sort these in chronological order and be sure to carry forward any unused receipts from last year. Create a "fiscal year" with at least one month in the 12-month period ending in the current tax year. This may create a better claim for you than the calendar year and help you recover some tax benefits from last year's expenses. Remember to reduce all medical expenses by any reimbursements from your medical plans, and the total by 3% of your net income to a maximum of $1,614. Also remember that this effort might pay off in the creation of a Refundable Medical Expense Supplement of up $500.

6. *Give to Your Favourite Charity Before Year End:* If you give, by December 31 of the current year, you'll speed up your tax benefits by claiming them on the tax return you'll file this spring. If you wait to give in January of the new year, you'll have to wait until you file next year's return to reap any tax rewards.

7. *Consider Political Contributions as a Tax Benefit:* By giving to your favourite political party by December 31, you receive a tax credit of $75 for the first $100 you give. A maximum credit of $500 can be claimed as a result of a contribution of $1,150. Both federal and provincial credits are available.

8. *Plan Asset Dispositions Carefully:* One of the most critical arguments for early year end tax planning is to match your potential capital gains and losses for the current tax year in order to minimize tax before dispositions. In general, capital losses can only be applied to capital gains of the year, not other income sources. However, you can choose to bring forward any previously unapplied capital losses to reduce capital gains you may be reporting, as an alternative to selling existing assets at a loss.

9. *Purchase Capital Assets:* For proprietors, late-year asset purchases can create capital cost allowance claims of one-half of the usual allowable rates. In the year of acquisition, you can receive a 30% write-off on half the acquisition costs of a new computer purchase, for example, or a new vehicle that was purchased before the end of the year. In 1998 there are also special tax breaks for businesses facing Year 2000 compliance.

10. *Reduce Tax on Pension Income:* If you are receiving periodic pension benefits from any pension sources, be sure to maximize your

allowable deductions for carrying charges, RRSP contribution room, or gifts to charities, in order to reduce the tax you must pay, and keep more of your Old Age Security and offsetting Age Amount.

11. *Plan Inter-Provincial Moves Carefully:* If you are changing province of residence, your income for the whole year will be taxed at the provincial rate applicable to your province of residence on December 31. A permanent move to Alberta from Manitoba, for example, should be contemplated before year end. Income for the whole year will then be taxed at the lower Alberta rates, resulting in a bigger tax refund. However, if you'll be moving from Alberta to Saskatchewan, consider spending New Year's in the mountains. A move early in the new year will save tax dollars on this year's return.

12. *Incur Operational Expenses Before Year End:* Sole proprietors and individual partners with a December 31 year end or certain commissioned salespersons who are eligible to claim expenses against their employment income, should consider making the following expenditures: fill up the gas tank, repair the car, purchase office supplies, install that business phone or fax line, or distribute those promotional flyers. Doing so before the year end will accelerate the tax benefits.

13. *Keep an Auto Log:* Make a resolution to record all business and personal driving during the year to maximize your claim for auto expenses. This is a simple procedure that will save you money during a tax audit. A good time to start is today!

14. *Log Unreceipted Expenses:* Don't forget to claim reasonable expenses for unreceipted amounts paid to wash your car at a coin car wash, for parking or for coin telephone calls.

15. *Keep Time Cards for Paying Your Children:* Commissioned salespeople and proprietors can claim the amounts paid to family members who have worked in the family business, provided proper documentation is kept and the work is actually performed at a rate you would normally pay a stranger.

16. *Don't File on the Wrong Tax Return:* Only the T1 General makes reference to all the tax deductions and credits you may be entitled to. Short forms may be simpler, but could cost you money in the long run. Plan to obtain the right return for your tax-filing profile.

17. *Get Your Refund More Quickly Using Direct Deposit:* To get the quickest possible refund from Revenue Canada, plan to file form T1DD and request that your refund cheque be deposited directly to

your bank account. The same arrangement can also be made for your Child Tax Benefit payments, the GST Credits and your public pensions. You may wish to make these arrangements in the new tax-filing year.

18. *Keep All Paper Documentation:* You must retain paper records supporting the figures on your tax return for a period of at least six years from the end of the year in which you received your Notice of Assessment. If Revenue Canada requests a review, you must produce these records, or your tax deductions will be disallowed.

19. *Do a Preliminary Tax Calculation:* The earlier in the year you can run through a tax calculation for your family, the better your chances of maximizing your RRSP contributions and other tax deductions to reduce your taxes payable. You'll also have several months to save up for a tax bill on April 30, to lessen the stress you'll feel if you wait until the last minute. Unhurried tax preparation paves the way to greater tax savings.

20. *Know When To Consult a Tax Professional:* Everyone should attempt to complete and understand his or her own tax return to make better "tax-wise" decisions during the year. However, a tax professional can help you save time and money in completing your return or in appealing assessment from Revenue Canada. Always ask for an estimate and evidence of a guarantee before you engage this individual or firm for this most important task. It may pay off handsomely over the long run to have a knowledgeable tax professional at your side to guide you to tax savings.

Note: Revenue Canada tells us that the No. 1 error made by Canadians is still mathematical. Check your computations carefully, or consider using tax software to help with this annual task.

INDEX